IN THESE
Difficult Times

IN **D**ifficult THESE **T**imes

RICHARD P. LINDSAY

Bookcraft
Salt Lake City, Utah

Library of Congress Catalog Card Number: 90-83208

ISBN 0-88494-758-0

First Printing, 1990

Printed in the United States of America

Contents

PART FOUR: *Spirit*

Preface

As with so many other observers of the contemporary scene, my professional experience and religious perspective have convinced me of the great and growing problems we face in our present society. One need not be an expert trained in diagnosing current social ills or measuring the impact of present trends in order to recognize the depth and breadth of the challenges we face and which, according to prophetic assurance, will intensify. Some of the most obvious include: sexual promiscuity, alcohol and drug abuse, child sexual abuse, pornography, and vandalism and violence in many forms. Such pathology is a predictable outcome of an increasingly secularized and despiritualized society with irreligion at its core.

If we continue our present course we can expect to experience more divorce, more depression, more suicide, and more emotionally disturbed youth. Age-old wisdom and current studies attest that the family is the most effective place to instill lasting values in its members and to provide the antidote to these grievous social ills. Where family life is strong and based on principles taught by the Savior, Jesus Christ, society moves forward and progress is assured. Where families fail, societies disintegrate.

In these challenging times many adults and especially the youth of this generation are victims of the persuasive and demoralizing influences that surround us all. We need only note the impact of a multi-billion-dollar pornography industry that so tragically afflicts our homes or the seductive motion picture and television fare that excites and gives license to promiscuous behavior. Nakedness or near nakedness has become the hallmark of much public entertainment. The pursuit of worldly pleasure is the passion of our time.

Personal freedom and family peace will increasingly become victims of the swamp of immorality that surrounds us as the evils of the world intensify. No family will enjoy peace nor will our lives be free unless our homes are built upon Christian principles of morality, fidelity, and mutual respect.

In this time of enveloping darkness and evil the simple, inspired teachings of the gospel can be the means of bringing us "out of darkness into his marvelous light." It is my hope that this book will serve to clearly identify not only the specific problems we face but also the gospel solutions that the Lord has made available to us.

As we face the frightening challenges in this dispensation of the fulness of times and also the dispensation of the fulness of evil, our hearts need not fail us. With the Lord's help and with wise, committed efforts to understand and apply the Savior's principles to these problems, we can be equal to the challenges we face.

This book is not an official Church publication, and I alone am responsible for the views expressed herein.

Acknowledgments

This effort bears the imprint of many religious, civic, and educational leaders who have blessed my life over the years.

Included in the list of such leaders who have heavily influenced my thought and preparation in this undertaking are President Gordon B. Hinckley, former President Hugh B. Brown, Elder Dallin H. Oaks, President Rex E. Lee, Dr. Agda Sophie Harlow, Dr. Harold L. Voth, Dr. Jerry R. Kirk, and countless others who in often humble, unassuming ways have touched my life by their teaching and example.

The detail of the book's preparation owes much to the painstaking efforts of Kathlene Beverley, Laurel D. Bailey, William S. Evans Jr., Leora S. Brockbank, Marye Burris, Mary Gifford, Joy Nelson, Kathleen E. Lubeck, Janet Thomas, and the editorial staff at Bookcraft.

The book is dedicated to the two women who have anchored my life and kept the faith "In These Difficult Times": Mary Powell Lindsay, my mother, who for forty-seven years of widowhood, rearing a large family as a single parent, never faltered, and taught her children to have faith; and my precious eternal companion of forty-one years, Marian Bangerter Lindsay, who has blessed my life beyond expression.

Society's Ills and the Savior's Way

And now, behold, I say unto you, that the thing which will be of the most worth unto you will be to declare repentance unto this people, that you may bring souls unto me, that you may rest with them in the kingdom of my Father'' (D&C 15:6).

In an earlier important segment of my life I would reflect daily upon the many human tragedies of our time. As the administrator of Utah's juvenile court system I observed constantly the havoc of young lives caught up in delinquency and neglect. These young people were often at war within themselves, with their families, and with society in general. Later, when I served as the state director of the Council on Criminal Justice, I shifted my perspective to the tremendous toll of tragedy and suffering adult crime causes to individuals, families, and society. Still later I served as executive director of a number of combined state agencies dealing with problems of the human condition, including the departments of health, welfare, mental health, drugs and alcoholism, and corrections.

Although it would be unrealistic to oversimplify the many causes and tragic consequences of the diverse human problems and conditions which brought about the need for these public agencies, from these associations I was led to three fundamental conclusions. First is the overwhelming public cost and human tragedy resulting from the great health, social, and emotional problems of our time.

Second, it is obvious that remaking society will be accomplished only through our understanding, teaching, and living those redeeming principles taught by Jesus of Nazareth.

Finally, the family is the God-given laboratory in which to accomplish the major teaching and living of these divine principles. The Christ-centered family, founded on principles of love, sharing, fidelity, compassion, mutual support, and kindness, is clearly the Lord's answer to the problems of our time.

I recall a conversation I had by telephone with my daughter Susan, who lives with her family in suburban Washington, D.C. For the previous three years she had lived in the Far East with her husband, who was an assistant to the U.S. ambassador of Beijing, China. During the uprising by students and other elements of Chinese society which culminated in the bloody climax in Tiananmen Square in May 1989, Susan, with other dependents of embassy personnel, was required to leave her apartment with her three sons on less than one hour's notice. Her hurried return to her homeland was an experience she will long remember.

In our conversation I said, "Susan, you must feel grateful to be back on American soil after such a challenging and emotional experience." Her response was not what I had anticipated. "Of course we are grateful to be home, Dad. It is such a blessing to be back in our own free country. But you know, I now live in the 'murder capital of the world.' In some ways I feel less real personal security than when I lived in the Far East."

It was a sobering response, and I have often reflected on her comments. Any thoughtful observer of the contemporary scene in the United States cannot help but be increasingly concerned and even discouraged by the precipitous slide in the moral, spiritual, and ethical values and behavior in our country.

It is estimated that nearly one-third of all homes in the United States are victimized by some form of criminal activity *each year*. During 1989 in the United States more than 30,000 people were killed by criminals — more than five times the number of Americans killed each year in the Vietnam War. A survey from *Newsweek* magazine reported that 53 percent of all Americans are afraid to walk at night in some areas within a mile of their homes.

Crime and delinquency in this country have been conservatively estimated as amounting to more than $125 billion a year in direct costs. A by-product of this sobering statistic is a nation increasingly frightened and demoralized by criminal activity. The vast resources we commit each year to law enforcement, the courts, correctional institutions, rehabilitation, and crime prevention efforts have not curtailed the surge of crime. Estimates of the direct costs of AIDS, venereal diseases, alcoholism, and drug abuse, which when combined total well in excess of $50 billion a year, add further evidence to the tragic picture of the nation's ominous moral decline.

We could add mountains of additional data to document this precipitous moral slide our country has experienced in recent years. We know that large numbers of abortions take place each day, and in addition many babies are now born to unwed mothers. AIDS, a sexually transmitted disease, continues to spread as an epidemic.

Many times it is the innocent who suffer as a result of these social ills. Elder Boyd K. Packer has said:

> The bodies and minds and morals of increasing numbers of little children are brutalized and abused by those who should protect them.
>
> In it all, mankind has sown a bitter wind and reaps heartbreak, guilt, abandonment, divorce, addiction, disease, and death; and little children suffer.
>
> If these sins remain unchecked, civilization will be led unfailingly to destruction. ("Little Children," *Ensign,* November 1986, pp. 16–17.)

Profound changes are taking place in the structure of the society in which we live. Many values and traditions that provided health and stability to our way of life are being overthrown, and new life-styles are being blindly followed as if they were divinely prescribed. Perhaps no institution has come under heavier assault than the family. The divorce rate for first-time marriages in the United States approaches 50 percent, with even higher divorce rates for subsequent marriages. Many other marriages, although legally intact, are little more than part-time families, with both parents largely gone from the home and traditional family life virtually nonexistent.

The ominous changes taking place in our society, and especially in the American family, must be forthrightly addressed if our society is to continue as we have known it. The values people live by are largely a function of the family life they experienced in growing up. Healthy, mature adults raised in an atmosphere of a quality family life embrace solid, constructive values, and society moves forward. Sick people embrace sick values, and society is weakened. The pivotal role in this process is the family. Good parenting requires our greatest commitment, for the very fate of mankind depends upon it. And it is clear that, without such a commitment, the vitality of our society will inevitably decline as the number of individuals increase who cannot fully shoulder the responsibilities of life—especially family life.

Time remaining to change the nation from its course of self-destruction is running out. Restoring the stability of the family and developing wholesome family relationships must be the concern of us all. It is interesting to note that only seventeen generations have passed since Columbus set foot on American soil. Some analysts of our society have projected that, if present trends and the present rate of disintegration continue, three or four more generations may see the destruction of our way of life. Symptomatic of this downward trend is the rearing of a generation that continually wishes to be given to—rather than to give.

Clearly members of The Church of Jesus Christ of Latter-day Saints must be concerned with the social problems I have enumerated. The real question is, What can be done about it?

We would do well to review the life of the Savior and study the ways in which he reacted to such problems when he was on the earth during his mortal ministry. Severe social problems, disease, poverty, thievery, and bondage were also products of his era. His parable of the good Samaritan, a story which involved a brutal attack on a lone traveler, could have been taken from a real happening of his time or our time. He was profoundly touched by man's inhumanity to man.

Above all, the Savior knew that change in the individual was essential to bring about a change in society. This change in an individual's actions is brought about by a change in his spirit, and change in his spirit comes from the acceptance of God and applying His commandments.

In the Book of Mormon we have a classic example of how the gospel can be applied to cure men's ills. Finding that the government which he led could not reduce the crime and inequality among his people, Alma resigned his leadership as chief judge and went forth to change his people by teaching God's ways: "And now, as the preaching of the word had a great tendency to lead the people to do that which was just—yea, it had had more powerful effect upon the minds of the people than the sword, or anything else, which had happened unto them—therefore Alma thought it was expedient that they should try the virtue of the word of God" (Alma 31:5). Alma did not disavow the importance of his judicial office, but he recognized the need for men's hearts to change if their lives were to change for the better.

In the golden era that followed Christ's appearance on the American continent, the effect of applying His teachings was profound.

> And they had all things common among them; therefore there were not rich and poor, bond and free, but they were all made free, and partakers of the heavenly gift. . . .
>
> And there were no envyings, nor strifes, nor tumults, nor whoredoms, nor lyings, nor murders,

nor any manner of lasciviousness; and surely there could not be a happier people among all the people who had been created by the hand of God. (4 Nephi 1:3, 16.)

In our day the Church proclaims that the remedy for social ills lies in the doctrines and principles the Church teaches. Note the spirit of the gospel in these words:

Remember the worth of souls is great in the sight of God;

For, behold, the Lord your Redeemer suffered death in the flesh; wherefore he suffered the pain of all men, that all men might repent and come unto him.

And he hath risen again from the dead, that he might bring all men unto him, on conditions of repentance.

And how great is his joy in the soul that repenteth!

Wherefore, you are called to cry repentance unto this people.

And if it so be that you should labor all your days in crying repentance unto this people, and bring, save it be one soul unto me, how great shall be your joy with him in the kingdom of my Father!

And now, if your joy will be great with one soul that you have brought unto me into the kingdom of my Father, how great will be your joy if you should bring many souls unto me! (D&C 18:10–16.)

You cannot permanently help a man if you cannot encourage him to change in his attitude toward God and mankind. The Church does not merely convert men to Christ. The Church has a program that transforms belief into action, first to effect a change in the convert himself and then to harness his enthusiasm and energy in extending his new-found way of life to others.

There is a genuine concern in the Church for those deprived of the comforts of life, for the victims of social injustice or crime, for the sick and the afflicted, and for the tragic consequences of broken families. But there is a remedy which must be brought to all mankind. This remedy offered to all of God's children is that if they will come unto Jesus, if they will accept and practice the pure love of Christ, they will find the peace on earth he promised them.

This can come only by a transformation within the individual soul—a life redeemed from sin and brought into harmony with the divine will. Instead of demonstrating selfishness, God's children must give their abilities, their possessions, their fortunes, their sacred honor, and their lives, if necessary, for the alleviation of the ills of mankind. Hate must be supplanted by sympathy and forbearance. Peace and true prosperity can come only by conforming our lives to the law of love, the law of the principles of the gospel of Jesus Christ. A mere appreciation of the social ethics of Jesus is not sufficient—men's hearts must be truly changed!

As we assess the ills of the society in which we all live and which are detailed in the chapters that follow, the Savior's way becomes the clear and unmistakable solution to the problems of our time.

PART ONE _____

Society

The Pornography
Threat to America

Pornography is one of the problems in our land whose direct dollar costs and indirect costs in human suffering and degradation are staggering and beyond calculation. Contrary to the view expressed by some, pornography *does* hurt. It debases society, and its growing influence threatens our view of life and opposes all that true religion teaches about human relationships. As pornography has grown in popularity, its content has worsened considerably. Much of it now portrays violence, degradation, and humiliation in addition to explicit sexual content. Common pornographic themes now include sadism, incest, child molestation, rape, and even murder.

So-called adult bookshops in the United States now total more than fifteen thousand—three times the number of the nation's largest restaurant chain. The industry is estimated to take at least $8 billion per year, almost as much money as conventional movie and record industries combined.

There are estimated to be more than four hundred pornographic magazines on the market in the United States. More than twenty million men and boys purchase them regularly. Similarly at least two to three million Americans view pornographic movies each week. Videotapes of such films are said to represent up to 50 percent of the home movie market. According to 1981 statistics, one well-known pornographic film alone sold more than three million video copies at approximately six dollars each, for a total of $18 million.

It is the right and responsibility of our nation to maintain a decent society and to enact and influence those laws which seek to stem the tide of commercialized obscenity. In an important decision, the United States Supreme Court held "that there are legitimate state interests in stemming the tide of commercialized obscenity" (*Paris Adult Theater v. Slaton*).

A study in which the Michigan State Police Department used a computer to classify over 35,000 sex crimes committed in that state over a twenty-year period concluded that in 43 percent of the crimes pornography was rated as a major antecedent cause (*Christian Life*, March 1981, p. 60).

Large sections of some of our nation's largest and most beautiful cities have become crime-ridden wastelands in the wake of saturation and infestation by pornography establishments of every description.

The past decade has witnessed a puzzling paradox in our land. Poll after poll clearly indicates that the vast majority of Americans believe pornography is morally wrong, and that it debases society and ought to be controlled—and controlled more strictly than it has been in the past. The polls have remained remarkably consistent over the years.

Yet we find greater and greater inroads being made by the smut merchants, and with breathtaking speed. What was considered by many to be unthinkable depravity a decade ago is in the mainstream of pornography today. If we predict the future based upon our descent of the past ten years, we in America are in serious trouble.

Not many years ago, a person trying to defend pornography would have felt impelled to bring up philosophical arguments, Supreme Court rulings, and pseudoscientific studies from extremely liberal countries in an effort to prove that pornography was not harmful. Speakers who defended pornography often did so with a degree of embarrassment and took great pains to point out that they were defending a concept, but that they themselves did not purchase or view any pornography, nor would they allow it into their own homes.

It is a sad commentary that circumstances have changed to the extent that now it is the speaker opposed to the current proliferation of pornography who must try to prove that pornography is wrong.

The fact is that within the short space of a decade or so, the mores of our society have changed drastically. Many millions who consider themselves self-respecting Americans think nothing of playing X-rated videotapes in their homes, or of purchasing magazines which only recently they themselves may have called filthy, or of permitting their children to listen to records which warp minds and distort reality.

Pornography is wrong. It is dangerous and it is harmful. Pornography destroys human sensitivity. It adds a certain callousness to the observer. It blunts his or her sense of moral outrage. It attacks the ability to judge right from wrong. Of greater concern, it creates a distorted view of reality in the observer and thereby complicates pre-existing personal problems. Moreover, viewing pornography can produce unnecessary tensions in otherwise healthy marriages. The proliferation of pornography has undoubtedly been a factor in the increased divorce rate. It has made premarital and extramarital sex more acceptable, and it has cheapened women to the extent that a great many men identify women as sex objects rather than as persons worthy of respect.

Let me refer briefly to an Associated Press release carried in the *Deseret News* on 14 February 1983:

> Convicted murderer Theodore Bundy, in a book to be published later this month, discusses the motives of the "protokiller" who committed the crimes for which he was convicted.
>
> But the book's authors firmly believe that Bundy's comments—taken in a series of interviews taped between March 1980 and March 1981 on Florida's death row—draw a self-portrait. . . .
>
> Bundy, convicted in the 1978 slaying of a 12-year-old Lake City [,Florida,] girl and the beating deaths of two Florida State University sorority sisters the same year, was careful to speak in the third person throughout the interviews. . . .
>
> Bundy was convicted in 1976 in Salt Lake City of kidnapping a 17-year-old girl from a shopping mall. . . . Bundy was [also] investigated in the slayings of three 17-year-old Utah girls. . . .
>
> The 36-year-old former University of Utah law student told how juvenile fantasies fed by pornographic magazines and sexy suntan commercials

led his "protokiller" to X-rated movies and book-stores.

Bundy, who authorities believe may have killed 21 young women between 1974 and 1978, said crime stories would fascinate "this person," and that the central thrill for him in pornography was not sex, but the abuse and possession of women as objects.

Pornography has fueled a degradation in the value of humanity itself. The fact that child pornography could demand so large and lucrative a market is but one indication of this fact. Pornography is a corrosive influence, and society can no longer look at the burgeoning spread of pornography from a totally objective point of view. Rather we should act to eliminate pornography through appropriate legal means in much the same way that we outlaw other unacceptable, aberrant, or deviant behavior patterns.

At this point those who would protect the position of pornographers inevitably trot out the Constitution of the United States. "Don't touch," they say. "You dare not abridge the right of free speech or freedom of the press." This, of course, raises the natural question of whether the framers of the Constitution intended to protect the rights of pornographers to purvey their wares in the guise of "free speech." Rather, I believe, they intended to protect the right to state ideas, to project values, to interact, to criticize, to influence, to debate, without restrictions. Pornography fits into none of the above categories.

If pornography is a means of communication, if obscenity is to be protected as a form of free speech, then logically it might be argued that the acts depicted in pornographic material should themselves be protected by the First Amendment. If such logic is sustained, we may see the day not long hence when the First Amendment will be employed to protect the rights of individuals executing flagrantly obscene acts in public.

I do not lay claim to an exhaustive knowledge of constitutional law, but I do believe that as parents we have the inherent right to raise our children in a manner which leaves them free of a constant deluge of pornography in normal social relationships. As it now stands, the open display of pornographic materials in public places is, in my judgment, a clear invasion of our individual rights; it interferes with our ability to send our children into the street secure in the knowledge that they will not be exposed to perversely obscene materials with which they may have difficulty in coping.

Officials charged with implementing and interpreting the law in some of our country's largest cities seem to be saying, "If you do not want to be exposed to pornography, you are perfectly free to avoid certain streets or to simply close your eyes." I sometimes wonder what the reaction would be if one were to arrange to deliver an hour-long religious message over a public address system on those same streets. Most likely it would be loudly opposed by those who object vehemently to being intruded upon and who would not be mollified by the suggestion that they need only close their ears.

Across the nation, women and men are becoming increasingly vocal in fighting pornography, and in many cases their efforts have succeeded. Under the First Amendment, one has the right to say and by his actions to demonstrate that he doesn't like pornography. It is pornography—not the outcry against it—that violates women's, children's, and men's constitutional right to life, liberty, and the pursuit of happiness.

I do not want to have to close my eyes while walking the streets in my city or the streets of other great cities of our land. And I do not want to be a captive audience to those who traffic in commercialized pornography for selfish and greedy purposes.

As difficult as are the problems states and local communities have in trying to control pornography and obscenity, certain breakthroughs offer a glimmer of light at the end of the tunnel.

The United States Supreme Court, in the case of *New York v. Ferber,* upheld the right of the state of New York to prohibit child pornography. The Supreme Court determined that the New York statute which prohibits people from knowingly promoting a sexual performance by a child under the age of sixteen (by distributing material which depicts such a performance) is constitutional. The Supreme Court ruled that the statute in question does not violate the First Amendment.

Kentucky and Texas have passed strict child pornography laws which make it a felony to transfer any photograph or film of a child engaged in a sex act. With these laws, the pornography doesn't even have to be sold— just handed from one person to another. A tougher penalty for a felony conviction has drastically reduced the flow of child pornography in these states.

North Carolina enacted a single-use law that allows only one kind of "adult entertainment" in a building. Thus an X-rated movie theater may not sell dirty books, or an adult bookstore run automated peep shows. This law also strikes at profits.

In several states, such as North Dakota, Iowa, Wisconsin, and Colorado, where new obscenity legislation is being proposed, legislators have included conditions restricting X-rated drive-ins from showing films within two thousand feet of a residence or within the viewing range of a juvenile. Some of the proposed laws have also stipulated that X-rated films may be shown only after 11:00 P.M.

But legal loopholes occur, and many communities have enacted their own ordinances to stop hard-core pornography locally.

In San Diego, California, for instance, adult bookstores with peep-show booths must comply with strict fire codes. The walls must be fireproof, exits must be easily accessible, and aisles between the booths must be well lighted and wide.

The cities of Peoria, Illinois, and Miami, Florida, have enacted license or permit regulations to control X-rated movie theaters and bookstores. One of the biggest problems in prosecuting hard-core pornographers is proving ownership, and license regulations provide a first step in tracking down the owners: the person applying for the permit must give his name and address. Another advantage to this type of ordinance is that the permit can be revoked if the business becomes a trouble spot.

Many areas have laws prohibiting the display of sexually explicit material in newsracks, store windows, and other easily viewed places. Some communities also require that cable TV stations be subject to local and state obscenity laws. Other municipalities are simply barring the broadcast of X-rated films.

Milwaukee has enacted a city ordinance aimed at controlling indecent and obscene material of cable TV programming. In the ordinance, indecent material is clearly defined as a representation or verbal description of a human sexual or excretory organ or function or of nudity which under contemporary community standards for television is patently offensive. The violation of any of the provisions of the ordinance, upon conviction, brings a fine or imprisonment.

Cleveland's ten-year effort to enforce Ohio's obscenity laws was upheld on 4 February 1982, with the decision of the United States Courts of Appeals for the Sixth Circuit upholding the Ohio Obscenity Statute.

Let me offer some suggestions on how you can help stop pornography in your own communities.

Sponsor community forums and seminars to educate residents as to what hard-core pornography is, its dangers, and how it can be stopped. You may want to begin with a trusted and competent officer from your local police department who can explain to you the various types of pornography. Speakers are also available from organizations that fight pornography.

Review local obscenity laws. Are they effective? Do they need revision? Are the penalties severe enough?

Tell lawmakers how you feel about obscenity. Offer to help by evaluating the types of laws that are effective elsewhere.

Tell your mayor and police commissioner or chief that you want local police officers trained in methods for gathering evidence and making solid arrests on obscenity charges. Emphasize that you'll be watching for progress.

Let your district attorney know that you want obscenity cases prosecuted to the full measure of the law.

Stop the delivery of unsolicited sexually explicit mail to your home in the United States by filling out form 2201 at your local post office. After thirty days from the date your name is added to the reference list, anyone who sends you sexually oriented advertisements subjects himself to legal action by the government.

We recognize that pornography is a drastic problem in our nation. Countless lives are affected adversely by this spreading epidemic of immorality, violence, and perversion. In efforts to oppose pornography and obscenity, however, let us realize that the greatest deterrent to these ills is one that provides young people with the opportunity to fill their lives with healthy, positive alternatives to pornography. The most effective of these efforts, as the Church teaches, are home-based and parent-centered.

A better tomorrow begins with the training of a better generation. This places upon parents the responsibility to do a more effective work in the rearing and guiding of their children. The home is the place where character is best formed and habits established.

You know that your children will learn to read. They will read books and they will read magazines and newspapers. Cultivate within them a taste for the best. While they are very young, read to them the great stories which have become immortal because of the virtues they teach. Expose them to good books, including at least a few books of the kind upon which great minds have been nourished.

Let there be *good* magazines about the house which will stimulate their thoughts and interests. Encourage them to read a good newspaper so that they may know what is going on in the world. When there is a good movie in town, consider attending the theater as a family; your very patronage will give encouragement to those who wish to produce this type of entertainment. And use very carefully that most remarkable of all tools of communication, television, to enrich their lives. There is much that is good there, but it requires great selectivity. Let those who are responsible for good family entertainment know of your appreciation for that which is good, and also of your displeasure with that which is bad. In large measure, we get what we ask for. The problem is that so many of us fail to ask and, more frequently, fail to express gratitude for that which is good.

There should be good music in the home. If you have teenagers who have their own recordings, you may be prone to describe the sound as something other than music. Expose them to something better so they have a real basis for choosing. Good music will speak for itself. More appreciation will come than you may think. It may not be spoken, but it will be felt, and its influence will increase as the years pass.

To counteract the impact and exposure of obscenity and pornography on our own children, caring, concerned, committed parents are the best answer to this threat to our young people. In combatting this problem, we would do well to remember the wise teaching of President Harold B. Lee, who said that the greatest work we will do will be within the walls of our own homes.

The battle against pornography is sometimes a lonely battle against entrenched and powerful forces. But whatever the odds, there is great satisfaction in being on the right side in the battle which engages us all.

The Case for Chastity

Our Church leaders recognize that the youth of the Church are surrounded by unbelievably great pressures from the media and from peers to follow negative role models and to express sexual feelings. We live in an environment where sex exploitation is epidemic, where all too often music, television, movies, books, and magazines send the message that whatever satisfies one's desires and feels good is okay. Tragically, responsibility to one's self, one's present or future partner, and even to unborn children is ignored.

May I briefly suggest a few indicators that demonstrate the tragedy and seriousness of the moral deterioration that has taken place in our nation.

In many American cities, including our nation's capital, abortions outnumber live births. In 1986 more than one million unmarried young women in the United States had babies. According to surveys taken around this same time period, nearly 60 percent of high school students in America had lost their virginity, as had 80 percent of college students. (See "What's Gone Wrong with Teen Sex," *People*, 13 April 1987, p. 111.)

The following appeared in the 21 May 1987 issue of the *Wall Street Journal:*

> AIDS [appears to be reaching] plague[like] proportions. Even now it is claiming innocent victims: newborn babies and recipients of blood transfusions. It is only a matter of time before it becomes widespread among heterosexuals. . . .
>
> AIDS should remind us that ours is a hostile world. . . . The more we pass ourselves around, the larger the likelihood of our picking something up. . . .
>
> Whether on clinical or moral grounds, it seems clear that promiscuity has its price. (P. 28.)

We could discuss many other indicators of our nation's moral deterioration. However, let us instead study the teachings of our prophet and our leaders on the ways in which the Lord's teachings and our own personal moral discipline can address some of these overwhelming problems of moral decay. What can be done to help curb this great human tragedy? To attack the root of the problem, we need to understand and teach that young people *can* control their desires for premarital physical intimacy.

No apology need be made for the teaching and practice of premarital sexual abstinence. It is the most viable, realistic approach to the problems of teen sex, out-of-wedlock pregnancy, and the growing AIDS epidemic.

President David O. McKay said that a necessary ingredient of spirituality is a "consciousness of victory over self" ("Man—the Jewel of God," *Improvement Era,* December 1969, p. 31). Two great blessings that can come from chastity are self-mastery and self-knowledge.

The letter of the law of chastity is to have sexual experiences only with one's spouse, the man or woman with whom legal marriage covenants have been made. But the spirit of this law encompasses far more. It requires that we keep sacred and appropriate all of our sexual desires—and all related behaviors. The sexual drive is given to man from God, but for man to constantly dwell upon it is inappropriate. This is lust—the mental pursuit of that which is spiritually damaging.

Lust causes one to draw attention away from that which is spiritually productive and fulfilling—to focus upon nonfulfilling and spiritually damaging thoughts and actions. It is a mental narcotic that causes us to lose sight of our long-range goals. It can lead us to sacrifice for a momentary experience all that is valuable, and it can leave us with nothing but pain and sorrow and confusion.

To fully give ourselves to the Lord, we must first have control of ourselves. Discipleship requires discipline. We can come to fully know and love God only as we live the kind of life he has set for us. Chastity, as much as any other gospel principle, helps us to know God because it promotes essential godly qualities such as understanding, self-mastery, love, and compassion.

The truth is that chastity is a godly virtue, and "the natural man receiveth not the things of the Spirit of God: for they are foolishness unto him: neither can he know them, because they are spiritually discerned" (1 Corinthians 2:14). Consequently, only those who are spiritually sensitive can understand spiritual things. Thus the world in its natural state will never fully understand why we place so much importance on living the law of chastity.

Some have taught that intimate sexual experiences within marriage are a necessary evil. Prophets have told us this is not so. Such experiences, when enjoyed in accord with God's commandments and the Spirit, can enrich one's life and enliven the soul. President Kimball referred to conjugal relationships in marriage as "inherently good" ("The Lord's Plan for Men and Women," *Ensign,* October 1975, p. 4). Quoting Billy Graham, President Kimball also said, "Sex can be a wonderful servant but a terrible master: . . . it can be a creative force more powerful than any other in the fostering of love, companionship, happiness" ("Guidelines to Carry Forth the Work of God in Cleanliness," *Ensign,* May 1974, p. 8).

Jeffrey R. Holland has taught:

Human intimacy, that sacred, physical union ordained of God for a married couple, deals with a symbol that demands special sanctity.

Such an act of love between a man and a woman is—or certainly was ordained to be—a symbol of total union: union of their hearts, their hopes, their lives, their love, their family, their future, their everything. It is a symbol that we try to suggest in the temple with a word like *seal.* . . .

. . . Such a total, virtually unbreakable union, such an unyielding commitment between a man and a woman, can come only with the proximity and permanence afforded in a marriage covenant, with the union of all that they possess—their very hearts and minds, all their days and all their dreams. They work together, they cry together, they enjoy Brahms and Beethoven and breakfast together, they sacrifice and save and live together for all the abundance that such a totally intimate life provides such a couple. And the external symbol of that union, the physical manifestation of what is a far deeper spiritual and metaphysical bonding, is the physical blending that is part of— indeed, a most beautiful and gratifying expression of—that larger, more complete union of eternal purpose and promise. . . .

. . . [The] symbolism of "one flesh" cannot be preserved, if we hastily and guiltily and surreptitiously share intimacy in a darkened corner of a darkened hour, then just as hastily and guiltily and surreptitiously retreat to our separate worlds—not to eat or live or cry or laugh together, not to do the laundry and the dishes and the homework, not to manage a budget and pay the bills and tend the children and plan together for the future. No, we cannot do that until we are truly one—united, bound, linked, tied, welded, sealed, married.

Can you see then the moral schizophrenia that comes from pretending we are one, sharing the physical symbols and physical intimacy of our union, but then fleeing, retreating, severing all such other aspects—and symbols—of what was meant to be a total obligation, only to unite again furtively some other night or, worse yet, furtively unite (and you can tell how cynically I use that word) with some other partner who is no more bound to us, no more one with us than the last was or than the one that will come next week or next month or next year or anytime before the binding commitments of marriage?

You must wait until you can give everything, and you cannot give everything until you are at least legally and, for Latter-day Saint purposes, eternally pronounced as one. To give illicitly that which is not yours to give (remember, "you are not your own") and to give only part of that which cannot be followed with the gift of your whole heart and your whole life and your whole self is its own form of emotional Russian roulette. If you persist in sharing part without the whole, in pursuing satisfaction devoid of symbolism, in giving parts and pieces and inflamed fragments only, you run the terrible risk of such spiritual, psychic damage that you may undermine both your physical intimacy and your wholehearted devotion to a truer, later love. You may come to that moment of real love, of total union, only to discover to your horror that what you should have saved has been spent and that only God's grace can recover that piecemeal dissipation of your virtue. (In Jeffrey R. and Patricia T. Holland, *On Earth as it is in Heaven* [Salt Lake City: Deseret Book Co., 1989], pp. 189–91.)

God is the same yesterday, today, and forever, and his covenants and doctrines are immutable; and when the sun grows cold and the stars no longer shine, the law of chastity will still be basic in God's world and in the Lord's church. The Church's stand on chastity is not an outworn garment, faded, old-fashioned, and threadbare. Old values are upheld by the Church not because they are old, but rather because through the ages they have proved right. It will always be the rule.

Illicit sex is a selfish act, a betrayal, and it is dishonest. To be unwilling to accept responsibility is cowardly and disloyal. Marriage was meant to be an eternal covenant; fornication and all other deviations are for today, for the hour, for the "now." Marriage gives life; fornication leads to despair. Premarital sex promises what it cannot possibly produce or deliver. Rejection is often the fruit as it moves its participants down the long highway of repeated encounters.

Chastity is a principle of power. This positive principle helps us to understand ourselves, acquire spiritual power, build enduring relationships, and grow closer to God.

The gospel gives us a clear and wholesome perspective on chastity. That is especially obvious when gospel teachings are contrasted with teachings of the secular world. As one who has been blessed with more than forty years of the blissful companionship of a pure and virtuous daughter of God, I give you my own personal witness of the indescribable joy that God has promised in the covenant of eternal marriage—a relationship of joy and rejoicing here and the promise of its continuation forever.

Immorality and the Media

I fondly recall one Saturday morning when I was blessed to perform the temple sealing of a young couple whose spiritual and temporal preparation and their understanding of this greatest event of their lives struck me as being exceptional.

Before the wedding, we visited in my office to discuss this sacred and beautiful event. After that visit, I rejoiced when I realized that even in these times, when the devastating forces of the adversary would subvert and pervert those eternal values we hold sacred, such choice spirits, with the nurture and support of wise, committed parents and the help of significant others in their lives, can face an eternal relationship pure and richly prepared.

As we visited, my mind went back thirty years to the

time when this young groom's own father and mother knelt at a similar altar in the same sacred temple. I was their bishop and Elder Harold B. Lee of the Council of the Twelve performed the same beautiful sealing ceremony. I could even recall some of the counsel and promises made by Elder Lee to this faithful couple who that day were beginning their own life's journey together.

And now this man's son was the young groom-to-be, preparing to complete a master's degree during the coming year. His bride would soon graduate with teaching credentials. He had fulfilled a successful and rewarding mission. Above all they reflected the good influence that caring loved ones and teachers had had on their lives.

As we concluded our visit together, we felt a spirit among us which caused us to weep for joy at the promise and blessings of the great eternal journey this choice, prepared, faithful young couple was about to embark upon.

In this dispensation the Lord has reiterated the commandment given at Sinai: "Thou shalt not . . . commit adultery, . . . nor do anything like unto it" (D&C 59:6). From the beginning of time, the Lord has set a clear and unmistakable standard of sexual purity. It always has been, it is now, and it always will be the same. That standard is the law of chastity. It is the same for all—for men and women, for old and young, for rich and poor.

In the Book of Mormon, the prophet Jacob tells us that the Lord delights in the chastity of his children (see Jacob 2:28). The Lord is not just pleased when we are chaste; he *delights* in chastity. Mormon taught the same thing to his son Moroni when he wrote that chastity and virtue are "most dear and precious above all things" (Moroni 9:9).

President Ezra Taft Benson has counseled us as follows:

My dear brothers and sisters, the law of chastity is a principle of eternal significance. We must not be swayed by the many voices of the world. We must listen to the voice of the Lord and then determine that we will set our feet irrevocably upon the path He has marked.

The world is already beginning to reap the consequences of its abandonment of any standards of morality. As just one example, recently the secretary of the Department of Health and Human Services in the United States warned that if a cure for AIDS is not quickly found, it could become a worldwide epidemic that "will dwarf such earlier medical disasters as the Black Plague, smallpox and typhoid" ("HHS Chief Says AIDS Will Dwarf the Plague," *Salt Lake Tribune,* 30 January 1987, p. A-1).

As the world seeks solutions for this disease, which began primarily through widespread homosexuality, people look everywhere but to the law of the Lord. There are numerous agencies, both public and private, trying to combat AIDS. They seek increased funding for research. They sponsor programs of education and information. They write bills aimed at protecting the innocent from infection. They set up treatment programs for those who have already become infected. These are important and necessary programs, and we commend those efforts. But why is it we rarely hear anyone calling for a return to chastity, for a commitment to virtue and fidelity?

President Benson then added this additional warning:

> Do not be misled by Satan's lies. There is no lasting happiness in immorality. There is no joy to be found in breaking the law of chastity. Just the opposite is true. There may be momentary pleasure. For a time it may seem like everything is wonderful. But quickly the relationship will sour. Guilt and shame set in. We become fearful that our sins will be discovered. We must sneak and hide, lie and cheat. Love begins to die. Bitterness, jealousy, anger, and even hate begin to grow. All of these are the natural results of sin and transgression.
>
> On the other hand, when we obey the law of chastity and keep ourselves morally clean, we will experience the blessings of increased love and peace, greater trust and respect for our marital partners, deeper commitment to other, and, therefore, a deep and significant sense of joy and happiness. ("The Law of Chastity," *Brigham Young University 1987–88 Devotional and Fireside Speeches* [Provo, Utah: University Publications, 1988], pp. 50–51.)

As director of public communications for the Church I came to know something of the overwhelming influence of the media, especially television, in shaping our thoughts and values and our entire life-style. Let me share just a few figures which may be familiar to many of you, but which I believe will help us to better understand the urgency of this challenge.

In 1987 the average American home had the television set turned on an average of 7 hours and 7 minutes each day. The average viewer watched about 4 hours and 30 minutes each day, or 31.5 hours each week—

almost 19 percent of the waking and sleeping hours in a week. In contrast, Japanese and European viewers spend about 1 to 3 hours a day watching TV.

By the time our children graduate from high school they will have logged 16,000 hours of television viewing (including some 50,000 commercials), which is *more than all the hours spent in the classroom.*

Some studies indicate that children who are heavy viewers of television do worse in school than light viewers, that watching television depresses reading skills, restricts an expansion in language skills, and reinforces violent behavior.

In 1987 I asked our Church public communications staff to survey a typical day in the life of network television. They recorded 12 hours of programing on CBS for one day. For that one day there were:

— 84 scenes of violence, including 43 scenes of mindless destruction of property
— 25 scenes of physical abuse
— 1 scene of murder (low for some days)
— 15 scenes of verbal abuse
— 86 scenes using suggestive sexual material
— 9 scenes involving adultery or premarital sex
— 40 scenes that included extremely immodest dress, innuendo, or suggestive or vulgar jokes
— 1 scene of rape
— 36 scenes of suggestive sexual material used in advertising
— 45 scenes involving profanity

Projecting these numbers for all weekdays in a year, there would be:

— 21,840 scenes of violence
— 22,360 sexual scenes
— 11, 700 uses of profanity

And all of those scenes of violence, sex, and profanity occurred on *just one channel!*

The average numbers of such examples per hour were:

— 7 scenes of violence
— 7.2 scenes containing sexual material
— 3.8 uses of profanity

All this adds up to a total of 18 inappropriate scenes per hour, or one every 3 minutes and 30 seconds.

A 1987 National Council of Churches study of violence and sexual violence provided the following summary:

There is a causal relationship between viewing violence on television and subsequent aggressive behavior. A majority of studies demonstrates a positive association between aggressiveness and exposure to media violence.

Viewing of violent sexual materials stimulates aggression toward women and children. Also, violence portrayed stimulates sexual violence.

Most heavy viewers express a greater sense of insecurity and apprehension about their world.

The average child will have viewed some 150,000 violent episodes, including an estimated 25,000 deaths, by the time of his graduation from high school.

"Perhaps the most harmful messages TV brings into our homes relate to intimate physical relations," says Larry Tucker of Brigham Young University. He has done extensive research on this subject that documents what I believe we all intuitively sense:

In the past several years, there has been a marked increase in the frequency of flirtatious behavior and sexual innuendos on TV. Storylines and settings that include revealing or enticing apparel and explicit camera angles are on the increase. Moreover, references to intimate physical relations on TV, whether verbally insinuated or contextually implied, occur most often between unmarried partners—five times more frequently than between married couples. References to such relations with prostitutes come in second. Together, references to sexual conduct between unmarried partners and with prostitutes account for about 70 percent of all references to intimate physical conduct on television.

Male/female associations on TV tend to overemphasize the physical aspects of relationships. Couples tend to spend a disproportionate amount of time expressing love physically rather than through acts of kindness, sacrifice, and service. . . .

Also disturbing is the research that shows nearly 33 percent of all close relationships on TV involve conflict or violence. Relationships that are romantically linked tend to have the most conflict and violence—48 percent.

One expert [Elizabeth Roberts] has concluded: "Television is a sex educator of our children and a potentially powerful one. Contemporary television entertainment is saturated with . . . lessons which are likely to have an impact on young viewers' sexual development and behavior." ("What's on TV Tonight?" *Ensign*, February 1988, p. 20.)

President Gordon B. Hinckley in a 1987 conference address quoted from a letter he received from a concerned father:

One evening I was watching a TV movie with my sixteen-year-old son. When some crude language was used, I suggested that we turn off the TV. My son said, "All right, Dad, but that's nothing compared to what I hear at school all the time." In visiting with some of the youth in our community I receive the same report. One boy commented, "Everybody, nearly, talks that way. The girls are just as bad or worse than the boys."

What I fear from these reports is that the prevalent use of foul language has become an acceptable pattern in the schools, probably due in large part to the influence of TV and the general permissiveness in our society. Whatever the cause, I hope that some additional emphasis might be made to curb it, to help our youth appreciate the importance of proper language. (In "Take Not the Name of God in Vain," *Ensign,* November 1987, pp. 44–45.)

In an earlier conference address, President Hinckley quoted the following from a *Los Angeles Times* article written by John Dart and appearing in the 19 February 1983 issue:

A survey of influential television writers and executives in Hollywood has shown that they are far less religious than the general public and 'diverge sharply from traditional values' on such issues as abortion, homosexual rights and extramarital sex. . . . While nearly all of the 104 Hollywood professionals interviewed had religious background, 45 percent now say they have no religion, and of the other 55 percent only 7 percent say they attend a religious service as much as once a month.

In that same address, President Hinckley went on to comment:

These are the people who, through the medium of entertainment, are educating us in the direction of their own standards, which in many cases are diametrically opposed to the standards of the gospel. Even beyond these, who produce for public television and cable, are the hard-core pornographers who seductively reach out to ensnare those gullible enough and those so weak in their discipline of self that they spend money to buy these lascivious products. ("Be Not Deceived," *Ensign,* November 1983, pp. 45–46.)

Similarly, Elder Dallin H. Oaks has said: "I cannot remember when I first heard profane and vulgar expressions in common use around me. I suppose it was from adults in the barnyard or the barracks. Today, our young people hear such expressions from boys and girls in their grade schools, from actors on stage and in the movies, from popular novels, and even from public officials and sports heroes. Television and videotapes bring profanity and vulgarity into our homes." ("Reverent and Clean," *Ensign,* May 1986, p. 49.)

And in another conference address, Elder David B. Haight discussed this problem:

One of Satan's methods is to distract and entice us so that we will take our eyes off the dangerous crevasses. He has succeeded to such an extent that many no longer recognize sin as sin. Movies, television, and magazines have glorified sin into what they think is an acceptable life-style: "[fornication], adultery, incest, . . . serial marriages, drug abuse, violence and double-dealing of every imaginable variety, [that is] often portrayed as [normal] behavior; where people who do good are not . . . rewarded and those who do evil are not punished," so stated a *Los Angeles Times* writer (see *Salt Lake Tribune,* 9 Aug. 1986, p. C-7). ("Spiritual Crevasses," *Ensign,* November 1986, p. 37.)

President Ezra Taft Benson has said:

The Book of Mormon warns us of the tactics of the adversary in the last day: "And others will he pacify, and lull them away into carnal security, that they will say: All is well in Zion; yea, Zion prospereth, all is well—and thus the devil cheateth their souls, and leadeth them away carefully down to hell" (2 Nephi 28:21).

The plaguing sin of this generation is sexual immorality. This, the Prophet Joseph said, would be the source of more temptations, more buffetings, and more difficulties for the elders of Israel than any other (see *Journal of Discourses* 8:55).

President Joseph F. Smith said that sexual impurity would be one of the three dangers that would threaten the Church within—and so it does (see *Gospel Doctrine,* pp. 312-13). It permeates our society. ("Cleansing the Inner Vessel," *Ensign,* May 1986, p. 4.)

President Gordon B. Hinckley has written the following concerning the blessings of chastity:

Is there a valid case for virtue in our world? It is the only way to freedom from regret. The peace of conscience which flows therefrom is the only personal peace that is not counterfeit.

And beyond all of this is the unfailing promise of God to those who walk in virtue. Declared Jesus of Nazareth, speaking on the mountain, "Blessed are the pure in heart: for they shall see God" (Matthew 5:8). That is a promise, made by him who has the power to fulfill.

And again, the voice of modern revelation speaks an unmatched promise that follows a simple commandment:

"Let virtue garnish thy thoughts unceasingly." And here is the promise: "Then shall thy confidence wax strong in the presence of God. . . .

"The Holy Ghost shall be thy constant companion, . . . and thy dominion shall be an everlasting dominion, and without compulsory means it shall flow unto thee forever and ever." (D&C 121:45–46.) ("In Search of Peace and Freedom," *Ensign*, August 1989, p. 6.)

In a landmark address to seminary and institute teachers of the Church delivered at Brigham Young University on 11 July 1966, Elder Spencer W. Kimball gave this ringing challenge to some of the leaders of the Church. It has become only more prophetic with the passage of the intervening years. In that address he said:

My beloved brothers and sisters, I decided I would title my talk, "What I Want You to Teach My Grandchildren." May I express to you my appreciation for the powerful influence that you are having upon the sons and daughters of Zion. I find the missionaries who come through this program are the better adjusted and more faithful ones, and the homes which have had your influence are the more righteous ones.

Every week I meet with the bishoprics, stake presidencies, and other leaders. I make the bold statement that if their normal boys go into the mission field well prepared, their marriage problems will be largely solved in advance. Practically all such fortified young men will marry in the temple without pressures or follow-up. It will follow as the day the night. I observe the shades of darkness dissipating when I see well trained young men marching toward their mission fields. Then upon their return in due time moving toward the temple in their wedding trains. So I salute you, the trainers and inspirers of youth. Your responsibility is awesome. Your opportunities to become saviors near limitless.

We are constantly exerting ourselves to impress upon the parents of these, your myriad youth, that it is primarily parental responsibility to rear the children in faith and correct living, though we must be realistic and realize that many parents do fail in varying degrees to train their children. Therefore, all other agencies dedicated to doing good must pick up the torch. Chief of them all is the Church. . . . [The work of teachers of the gospel] cannot be mediocre. It must be brilliant and effective. . . .

The Church and its agencies and institutions constitute a little island in a great ocean. If we cannot hold the line and keep the floods of error and sin from entangling us and engulfing us, there is little hope for the world. Tidal waves of corruption, evil, deceit, and dishonor are pounding our shores constantly. Unless we can build breakwaters and solid walls to hold them back, the sea will engulf us and destroy us also. I hope you . . . will indoctrinate our youth to keep clean of mind and body and spirit. In the old days of the Saturday night bath only, there were body odors and feet odors and halitosis, but now we worry little about these when showers and tubs and swimming pools are available to most of our young, and when nearly every child is trained to brush his teeth, keep his clothes clean, and shampoo his hair. How I wish all children were so well trained in the moral field. Our worries for hair and body and teeth are reduced, but there are other odors which are repugnant. I hope you will teach your charges to keep their minds as clean and their spirits as free from ugly odors involving morals. The stench of obscenity and vulgarity reaches and offends the heavens. It putrifies all it touches.

It is certain we cannot legislate goodness. It has been tried. We cannot depend upon lawmakers or judges to protect us. We cannot totally control theft or burglary or rowdyism or brutality or immorality or even murder with laws. Sometimes they act as a deterrent. The filth now reaching your youngsters through the mails of indecent pictures, articles and stories nearly drown them. It appears the only way we can give to our youth a peaceful clean survival is to teach them before the tidal wave of the sewer engulfs them. We must build the walls before the storms come. We teach them correct principles. We ingrain them into their lives and then if they permit evil to swamp them, at least we have done our part. Would you please help the youth of Zion to put on the whole armor of God?

In our efforts to improve our lives and the lives of our impressionable children, I hope we will be mindful of the tremendous influence that the media, particularly television, can have. Let us search out the good and the lovely; be careful not to allow unsupervised or indiscriminate television viewing; and be courageous enough to avoid those programs that can do untold damage to our moral sensibilities.

CHAPTER FIVE

Music—
Curse or Blessing

Adapting the words of Charles Dickens, we might say: "It is the best of times. It is the worst of times." We live during a time when more is available for our good and comfort than at any other time in the earth's history. However, as far as sin and corruption are concerned, we live in one of the worst times. Yet if we can remember the moving words of Joshua when our peers and others seek to have us choose music or any other thing that is contrary to godliness and goodness, we can still enjoy the best of times.

Joshua counseled, "Choose you this day whom ye will serve; . . . but as for me and my house, we will serve the Lord" (Joshua 24:15).

Lex de Azevedo, a widely known professional musician and composer and a former LDS bishop, made this thoughtful analysis of a major challenge of our time:

As society marches toward its last days, the conflict between good and evil intensifies. The gospel is spreading faster than ever before. We see more temples, more missionaries, more conversions, more nations opening to the gospel. Simultaneously, we see more sin, more pornography, more drugs, more violence, more broken homes, more immorality, and more degeneration of society in general. It should come as no surprise that the same elements found in society as a whole will be found in the art and entertainment media of our day. (*Pop Music and Morality,* [North Hollywood: Embryo Books, 1982], p. 67.)

Latter-day prophets have given us wise and enduring counsel on preparing our families for victory in this modern-day battle for the hearts, minds, and souls of our youth.

Music was given to us by a loving Heavenly Father. It can be a marvelous force for good. Inspiring music can fill the soul with heavenly thoughts.

President Kimball described in vivid detail the distinction between the Lord's holy purposes in the use of good music and the overwhelming influence and power of the adversary to use music to corrupt and destroy in the battle now raging.

Musical sounds can be put together in such a way that they can express feelings—from the most profoundly exalted to the most abjectly vulgar. Or rather, these musical sounds induce in the listener feelings which he responds to, and the response he makes to these sounds has been called a "gesture of the spirit." Thus, music can act upon our senses to produce or induce feelings of reverence, humility, fervor, assurance, or other feelings attuned to the spirit of worship. When music is performed in church which conveys a "gesture" other than that which is associated with worship, we are disturbed, upset, or shocked to the degree with which the musical "gesture" departs from or conflicts with the appropriate representation of feelings of worship. (*The Teachings of Spencer W. Kimball* [Salt Lake City: Bookcraft, 1982], p. 519.)

Brother de Azevedo has emphasized that it is a testimony to the incredible power of music that Satan has chosen it as one of the principal weapons in his latter-day arsenal. Though Satan can use music, he did not create it, for he is a destroyer and not a creator. Music was given to us by our Father in Heaven, and it is intended as a powerful force for good.

Music, then, is one of the great and holy gifts which our Father has given us for our blessing and joy. Satan, according to his nature, has labored to twist and corrupt this instrument of joy into an instrument of evil—even of death. It is always his work to spoil that which is finest and trick us into turning our life-giving powers against ourselves. But though Satan can tempt us to misuse this gift, its power for good remains and will remain forever.

Elder Ezra Taft Benson described the adversary's use of music and warned the youth of the Church: "The devil knows that music has the power to ennoble or corrupt, to purify or pollute. He will not forget to use its subtle power against you. His sounds come from the dark world of drugs, immorality, obscenity, and anarchy. His sounds are flooding the earth. It is his day—a day that is to become as the days of Noah before the Second Coming, for the prophets have so predicted. The signs are clear." (BYU Ten-Stake Fireside, Provo, Utah, 7 May 1972.)

On another occasion President Benson sounded this further warning:

> The Spirit of the Lord blesses that which edifies and leads men to Christ. Would his Spirit bless with its presence these festering [rock] festivals of human degradation . . . ? [The] music, crushing the sensibilities in a din of primitive idolatry, is in glorification of the physical to the debasement of the spirit. In the long panorama of man's history, these . . . rock music festivals are among Satan's greatest successes. The legendary orgies of Greece and Rome cannot compare to the monumental obscenities found in these cesspools of drugs, immorality, rebellion, and pornographic sound. . . .
>
> The Lord said, "For my soul delighteth in the song of the heart; yea, the song of the righteous is a prayer unto me" (D&C 25:12). It was pleasing unto the Lord where in Third Nephi . . . we read: "They did break forth, all as one, in singing, and praising their God" (3 Nephi 4:31). It was pleasing unto Satan when . . . Lehi's children and the "sons of Ishmael and also their wives began to make themselves merry, insomuch that they began to dance, and to sing, and to speak with much rudeness" (1 Nephi 18:9). (*God, Family, Country* [Salt Lake City: Deseret Book Co., 1974], pp. 248–49.)

As participants in the battle for the souls of young people, we must do more than "curse the darkness" of our time. Indeed, with prayer, judgment, and wisdom, there are many candles for us to light.

Elder Ezra Taft Benson quoted from Richard Nibley —a musician who for many years had observed the influence of music on behavior—as follows:

> Satan knows that music hath charms to soothe or *stir* the savage beast. That music has power to create atmosphere has been known before the beginning of Hollywood. Atmosphere creates environment, and environment influences behavior—the behavior of Babylon or of Enoch.
>
> Parents who retch at the radio and records reverberating in psychedelic revolt would do well to inventory their own record collection before complaining. If it is small, undiversified, and unused, the complaint must rest on the parent. Seeds of culture are best sown in the fertile ground of infant imitation. No amount of criticizing in the teen years can substitute for the young years of example that are lost. A parent who lost his chance to be a hero-image left a gap for a teen hero. (In "Satan's Thrust—Youth," *Ensign,* December 1971, p. 56.)

For young people to be in the world but not of the world has never been more difficult than it is today, but this burden must be shared by the parents.

The critical and complaining adult will be less effective than the interested and understanding one. Interest and understanding are only effective when they are genuine, and to be genuine they must be motivated by love. We must love our young people, whether they are walking in righteousness or even in error. In this way we can give them a chance to discern and to learn. But we must also give them a fair choice.

There comes a time when the general defilement of a society becomes so great that the rising generation is put under undue pressure and cannot be said to have a fair choice between the way of light and the way of darkness. As a result, today far too many are not choosing righteousness.

Parents and leaders of LDS youth need to have the power and the good common sense to give them a fair choice. As examples, we must be wise and cautious when choosing the type of music we listen to or musical performances we watch. Clearly, music is important in our lives and can be a wonderful, exhilarating form of entertainment. Equally clearly, some music can have a degrading or demoralizing effect. We must choose carefully before we ask our children to choose.

One solution to the current musical dilemma would be to flood the market with wholesome, edifying music. Why should we sit back idly and allow the adversary nearly total control of this powerful medium? As a people, we should contribute more to what today's youth, as well as adults, listen to; that is, we should be writing, composing, producing, and encouraging music that meets the Lord's approval and that will bless our lives. Latter-day Saint musicians and artists should be a leading force in creating more good original music as an antidote to much of the perverse musical fare that engulfs, especially, our youth.

Elder Boyd K. Packer has given some wise counsel about music and the control of our thoughts:

> Probably the greatest challenge to people of any age, particularly young people, and the most difficult thing you will face in mortal life is to learn to control your thoughts. As a man "thinketh in his

heart, so is he" (Proverbs 23:7). One who can control his thoughts has conquered himself. . . .

I want to tell you young people about one way you can learn to control your thoughts, and it has to do with music.

The mind is like a stage. Except when we are asleep the curtain is always up. There is always some act being performed on that stage. It may be a comedy, a tragedy, interesting or dull, good or bad; but always there is some act playing on the stage of the mind. . . .

If you can control your thoughts, you can overcome habits, even degrading personal habits. If you can learn to master them you will have a happy life.

This is what I would teach you. Choose from among the sacred music of the Church a favorite hymn, one with words that are uplifting and music that is reverent, one that makes you feel something akin to inspiration. . . . Perhaps "I Am A Child of God" would do. Go over it in your mind carefully. Memorize it. Even though you have had no musical training, you can think through a hymn.

Now, use this hymn as the place for your thoughts to go. Make it your emergency channel. Whenever you find these shady actors have slipped from the sidelines of your thinking onto the stage of your mind, put on this record, as it were.

As the music begins and as the words form in your thoughts, the unworthy ones will slip shamefully away. It will change the whole mood on the stage of your mind. Because it is uplifting and clean, the baser thoughts will disappear. For while virtue, by choice, *will not* associate with filth, evil *cannot* tolerate the presence of light.

In due time you will find yourself, on occasion, humming the music inwardly. ("Inspiring Music—Worthy Thoughts," *Ensign*, January 1974, pp. 27–28.)

Since music and other forms of entertainment have the potential to teach, inspire, inform, and entertain, but also the power to corrupt, degrade, and pervert, such entertainment has power to influence profoundly for good or evil all aspects of our values and feelings, as well as our behavior. We cannot remain unaffected by what we choose to expose ourselves to. Yet people of all ages are increasingly exposed to music and other forms of entertainment that can corrupt and pervert, as the following excerpt indicates:

"Social workers are almost unanimous in citing the influence of the popular media, television, rock music, videos and movies in propelling the trend toward pernicious sexuality. One survey has shown that in the course of a year the average viewer sees more than 9,000 scenes of suggested sexual intercourse or innuendo on prime time TV." (*Time*, 9 December 1985, p. 81.)

It is pleasing and refreshing to be able to turn from that depressing scene of wickedness to what the scriptures testify about the righteous power of music. The book of Job records that when the Lord laid the foundations of the earth, "the morning stars sang together, and all the sons of God shouted for joy" (Job 38:7). "O sing unto the Lord a new song," the Psalmist said. "Sing unto the Lord, all the earth." (Psalm 96:1.) "The Lord Jehovah is my strength and my song," wrote Isaiah (Isaiah 12:2). And again: "Sing, O heavens; and be joyful, O earth; and break forth into singing, O mountains" (Isaiah 49:13).

The Lord said to Emma Smith, through her husband, Joseph: "For my soul delighteth in the song of the heart; yea, the song of the righteous is a prayer unto me, and it shall be answered with a blessing upon their heads" (D&C 25:12).

On the night Jesus was born, his birth was announced by the song of angels. "And suddenly there was with the angel a multitude of the heavenly host praising God, and saying, Glory to God in the highest, and on earth peace, good will toward men" (Luke 2:13–14).

One of the last things Jesus did on this earth before going into the Garden of Gethsemane to make atonement for our sins—that single greatest event in the history of the universe—was to sing a song with his friends. Mark 14:26 notes, "And when they had sung an hymn, they went out into the Mount of Olives."

Music was just about the last thing the Prophet Joseph Smith enjoyed on this earth before he was murdered an hour or two later by a mob that broke into Carthage Jail and killed him and his brother Hyrum. Music in praise of Christ and in thanksgiving was the impression the spirits of those two martyr-heroes carried out of this world.

The war between good and evil rages on. We must choose sides and fight as best we can. Alma implored us, "Come ye out from the wicked, and be ye separate, and touch not their unclean things" (Alma 5:57). Much of today's music can undoubtedly be counted among those "unclean things."

When we consider the impact of music on us, and how many thousands of hours we listen to it throughout our lives, it is imperative that we choose for ourselves and our families music which builds up our spiritual reserves rather than that which continually wears them down. The Lord has cautioned us: "Let virtue garnish thy thoughts unceasingly" (D&C 121:45). Our abandonment of immoral music is only half the battle. As Richard Nibley indicated, encouraging and cultivating a taste for uplifting music in our homes is the necessary other half.

The War on
Alcohol Abuse

Alcohol abuse, with its addictive and destructive power, is a major problem in today's society. Treatment for alcoholism is at best difficult, yet through genuine, sincere family-centered efforts, the impact of alcohol as a major crippling force in our society can be significantly reduced.

Alcohol abuse, which seriously affects one in every five U.S. families, brings damaging social and spiritual consequences. The best and surest way to control it is abstinence.

Individually, we as Church members are encouraged to live the basic tenets of our faith and to maintain a proper balance between the spiritual, social, emotional, and physical aspects of life. Programs such as family home evening and home teaching offer important opportunities for family members to strengthen each other and for friends to offer support.

To assist Church leadership and social service professionals who are attempting to help Church families whose members may be afflicted with alcohol problems, the Church has published a resource manual to assist these families in coping with a wide variety of alcohol problems. This manual stresses the urgent need for concerned leaders and friends to help these persons stop drinking and to keep other family members from starting, and provides suggestions for helping families who are struggling with drinking problems.

Its main focus is on helping nondrinking family members. The ideas in the manual center around the use of resource people who are called by Church leaders and who use the training provided them to help individuals and families affected by alcohol abuse. They first gain the trust of the family and then present the discussions in the manual as the family needs them. Resource people may be home teachers who work with one or more families (under the direction of quorum leaders); visiting teachers who work with women in alcohol-impacted families (under the direction of the Relief Society president); or parents or other relatives who work with a teenager or other close relative.

In approaching the challenges faced by nondrinking family members, a resource person can help each family member:

1. Learn to respect himself and feel worthwhile.
2. Learn important communication skills that will lead to a happier, healthier family life.
3. Understand the effects of alcohol on the individual and the family.

4. Learn how to cope with problems caused by an alcoholic in the home.
5. Learn how to handle the stresses of life without using alcohol.
6. Prepare for full Church participation and spiritual conversion.
7. Develop new friendships by participating in Church-sponsored socials and meetings.
8. Leave drinking friends or other negative influences.
9. Learn ways to motivate alcoholics to get treatment.

When families learn these things, they will be more successful in helping their drinking loved one. Using the skills learned, they will be able to help the drinker to:

1. Recognize his problem.
2. Develop his own feeling that he needs to change.
3. Develop a sense of God's love and helpfulness.
4. Accept love and support from his family.
5. Use available resources to stop drinking.

With all our combined efforts to alleviate the terrible suffering and cost of alcohol abuse, the fact is that as a nation we are presently losing the war against this insidious social ill that plagues our society.

Two polls confirm this conclusion. A Gallup poll published in 1985 revealed that a growing number of American adults admit they sometimes drink more than they should, with 32 percent of drinkers in that particular survey acknowledging that they at least occasionally overindulge, compared to 23 percent in 1978 and 28 percent in 1974.

Another survey also showed that the proportion of people who say drinking has been a cause of trouble in their families remains at a high level. In 1985, 21 percent cited drinking as a family problem, compared to 18 percent in a July 1984 survey. The 1985 figure was nearly double the 12 percent recorded in 1974.

The *Washington Post* published a survey which revealed that young people, by a margin of 47 to 37 percent, tend to see alcohol as causing more problems in their communities than drugs do. Older Americans are more evenly divided, with 34 percent saying drinking is a bigger problem where they live, and 35 percent saying drugs are a bigger problem. Both groups, however, say that drinking has created more grief in their personal lives than have drugs.

One portion of the survey revealed an optimistic note concerning the growing national consensus for stronger alcohol control measures: "The public now endorses strong alcohol abuse measures. By 79 to 19 percent, those interviewed endorse legislation that would raise the legal drinking age in all states to 21, a measure aimed at reducing drunk driving among teenagers. Congress has ruled that by 1987, states that allow sales of liquor to people under 21 will risk losing federal highway funds."

Now, then, is the time for an intensive campaign against our nation's devastating health hazard of alcohol abuse. The time has come to give alcohol the same treatment that has produced a remarkable decline in tobacco consumption among Americans.

Among men aged 25 to 34, smokers have declined from 60 percent to 40 percent since the 1964 surgeon general's report on smoking and health was issued. This reduction of American male smokers is the direct consequence of an often fumbling and politically opposed effort to get the public to become aware of the toxic effects of smoking. But despite its limitations, it has been to a substantial extent successful, except among youth smokers, particularly young women.

All the health wreckage that has been reliably traced to tobacco is mild compared to that related to alcohol, whose devastation ranges from the killing and serious injury of thousands of innocent people on the highways to the commonplace self-destruction of careers and family relations.

As the effectiveness of the anti-tobacco campaign clearly shows, it is not necessary to *know everything* before you can *do something*. The public today appears highly receptive to reliable information about how to live longer in good health. This strongly suggests that it is time for an across-the-board barrage against the abuse of alcohol.

Our object should be to energize the good sense of the American people and encourage them to protect themselves and one another by remaking the image of drinking, just as has been done with smoking.

Cigarette advertising is barred from television, while alcohol consumption is permitted to be cleverly depicted in TV commercials as integral to good fellowship and joyous events. To the extent that the alcohol industry is under public attack for what it is selling, it responds with odes to moderation. But these actually are relatively infrequent, since the plague of alcoholism is widely accepted as a given of modern life.

In the interest of our nation's health, we must increase our efforts to inform, convince, and warn our fellow citizens of the terrible price we are paying for alcohol abuse.

The National Institute of Alcohol Abuse and Alcoholism, in its special report to Congress on alcohol and health in 1979 (and we know that the problem has increased since then), estimated that the excessive consumption of alcoholic beverages that year cost the United States more than $61 billion in the following categories:

Lost production	$28,026,280,000
Health and medical	18,179,980,000
Motor vehicle accidents	7,334,780,000
Violent crime	4,081,220,000
Social responses	2,768,380,000
Fire losses	613,610,000
	$61,004,250,000

The intervening years have only added to these estimated costs.

Perhaps these statistics are more striking if broken down into smaller units of measurement. An expanse of $61,004,250,000 per year means

$167 million per day,
$6.96 million per hour, or
$116,057 per minute.

The comptroller general of the United States stated in a 1983 report to Congress that the consumption of alcoholic beverages is the single largest factor in highway deaths, with some 25,000 people dying annually in accidents that involve drunk driving or that are in some way drinking related. Stated another way, that's nearly 500 people per week, or the equivalent of a loaded 747 passenger jet crashing each week and leaving no survivors. Can you imagine the furor that such frequent plane crashes would create in America and the demand that something be done?

If your family has been adversely affected by alcohol-related problems, you have a lot of company. More than one person in every five reports that alcohol has been a cause of trouble in his or her family. Again the 1985 Gallup poll cited earlier reported that 22 percent of adult

Americans say their homes are troubled by alcohol-related problems, nearly double the 12 percent recorded in 1974. Of particular concern for our nation's future is the fact that slightly more people under 30 years of age told Gallup interviewers that alcohol had caused trouble in their families than did people 30 years and older.

The long-term trends in alcohol consumption paint a grim picture of our nation's future unless we are somehow able to understand what is at stake in this continued erosion of our national health and well-being and to reverse these ominous trends. Utah, according to statistics, reports the lowest per capita total consumption of ethanol alcohol of all the fifty states in the United States. Even in this state, however, the costs of alcohol-related problems are frightening.

As a former chairman of our state legislature's Social Service Committee and earlier as the executive director of the State Department of Social Services, including health, mental health, welfare, corrections, drugs and alcoholism, and Indian affairs, I would submit that the greatest proximate cause of our staggering public expenditures for these human problem areas is alcohol abuse.

Current trends of increased per capita alcohol consumption can be reversed; indeed, they must be reversed if the present accelerated rate of wasting our nation's precious human and material resources is to be stemmed. We need to seek divine intervention in this battle against powerfully entrenched, well-financed forces who oppose efforts to reduce unwise consumption of alcoholic beverages.

In addition, however, we need to capture the minds and hearts of those millions of our sincere and caring countrymen who know of America's higher destiny and whose collective wisdom can be tapped in many practical ways to help turn the tide.

Many other initiatives are at hand to thoughtfully contain the spread of alcohol abuse. The Church has gone on record in the state of Utah with the following recommendations as deterrents to the continuing decay of home and family relationships from alcohol abuse:

1. Prompt further restrictions on the sale and distribution of alcoholic beverages.
2. Maintain the 21-year age requirement for legal sale or consumption of alcoholic beverages.
3. Promote restriction of the allowable modes and population targets of alcoholic beverage advertising, especially for minors.
4. Legislatively discourage the profit motive associated with the manufacture and sale of alcoholic beverages.
5. Provide a more strict enforcement of laws designed to discourage or restrict alcohol use, particularly those relating to liquor sales and driving under the influence.
6. Promote creative family-centered educational opportunities directed at the prevention of alcohol abuse. Abstinence should be included as a positive alternative in abuse prevention.
7. Promote the development of social priorities which will strengthen the place of families in the community and allow or encourage parents to assume rightful responsibility for their children.

While we labor to assist the families already suffering the impact of alcohol abuse, let us keep in mind our responsibility to help turn the tide against those forces in our society whose efforts are to increase alcohol consumption and thereby to increase the staggering problems caused by alcohol abuse.

PART TWO _____

Family

_____

CHAPTER SEVEN

The American Family
in Trouble

A revolution has occurred in American life during the past two decades that poses a greater threat to our country than the energy crisis, the national debt, or runaway inflation. If this revolution continues unabated, the inevitable result will be the progressive disintegration and ultimate collapse of our society. The revolution involves our misguided struggles to change and, in some cases, to destroy that most basic, most ancient, and most central of all human institutions: the family.

During this period in our country, the sacred bonds constituting the most basic human relationships have been systematically broken to the point that no human links of any kind are any longer regarded as inviolable.

An example of how swiftly the process of deterioration is occurring is found in the accompanying chart containing information from the U.S. Department of Commerce and printed in *U.S. News and World Report* (16 June 1980, p. 50). The chart summarizes changes in the American family in the ten-year period 1970–1980.

10 Ways Families Have Changed

	1970	1980	Percent Change	
Marriages performed	2,159,000	2,317,000	Up	7.3%
Divorces granted	708,000	1,170,000	Up	65.3%
Married couples	44,728,000	47,662,000	Up	6.6%
Unmarried couples	523,000	1,346,000	Up	157.4%
Persons living alone	10,851,000	17,202,000	Up	58.5%
Married couples with children	25,541,000	24,625,000	Down	3.6%
Children living with two parents	58,926,000	48,295,000	Down	18.0%
Children living with one parent	8,230,000	11,528,000	Up	40.1%
Average size of household	3.3	2.8	Down	15.2%
Families with both husband and wife working	20,327,000	24,253,000	Up	19.3%

The sixties were a decade of youth rebellion. The process of this rebellion began in part amidst the campus struggles in which a premium was placed on the ability and the willingness of young people to repudiate their parents and their parents' values. Adolescent rebellion, in a particularly bitter and enduring form, was elevated to the status of a permanent way of life. Parents, after periods of intense anguish, all too often had to reconcile themselves to permanent estrangement from their offspring. Children's feelings of resentment or even hatred towards parents and parents' similar feelings towards children were given social legitimacy. Children were usually the aggressors, but parents were by no means merely passive victims, and a good part of the problem stemmed from the recognition by the children that their parents were unwilling or unable to play the parental role and that the parents' own values were often hollow.

The seventies brought an unprecedented wave of divorce and of repudiation of marriage. Divorce is hardly a new phenomenon. However, only in the 1970s was divorce made to seem almost the natural climax of marriage. For a long time, despite the rising divorce rate, conventional wisdom held that marital breakdown was a catastrophe. Only in recent decades has a concerted and successful propaganda campaign been mounted which often treats divorce as a form of growth and progression.

More basic has been the denial of marriage itself, the refusal of so many people to enter into a formal contract with one another, precisely because they feel that the very idea of permanent commitment is unacceptable.

Finally, as children rejected their parents in the 1960s, parents rejected their children in the 1970s. Having children was now openly and respectably proclaimed a mere burden, and all sorts of strategies—from abortion to publicly funded day-care centers—were devised to eliminate that burden. By an appropriate kind of irony, as older people increasingly shirked the responsibilities of caring for the young, the young similarly rejected the burden of the old. Being elderly is already a bleak prospect, and by the end of this century it is likely to be even bleaker.

Just as in the 1960s many young people seem to have been angry primarily at adults who refused to be adults and who refused to relate to the young in such a way as to provide them with adequate guidance and appropriate models, so much of the anger and rejection directed at marriage and the family in the 1970s seemed to come from people who sensed that in many ways families had failed to be families, had instead become merely collections of people living in the same household.

Cries for help from distressed people are often indirect and stem from needs which the person in need does not fully understand. Thus, in the decade of the sixties, many young people desperately wanted to encounter strong and wise adults, but instead found only people eager to ape the young; and subsequently the youth responded by a bitter rejection of all of adult society, the defiant assertion that they wanted nothing to do with the adult world.

In later years and in our own time, the anti-family sentiments so ardently expressed have seemed often to come from people whose experiences of the family have been primarily of decay and disintegration; these individuals, therefore, can hardly allow themselves to believe that true families are even possible. It has become fashionable for many people to say that marriage represents merely a piece of paper and that liberated, modern people do not need the security which it represents.

Marriage does not exist primarily for the satisfaction of two people, however deeply committed they may be to one another. It is children who put the seal on that commitment, who forge it in such a way that much more is at stake than merely the desires of two people. It is in becoming parents that we fulfill a particular kind of destiny that God and nature have bestowed on most of us, and it is through parenthood that we achieve genuine adulthood.

Divorce itself is clearly the symptom rather than the cause of family distress. Sometimes it is the result of infidelity on the part of one or both partners to the marriage. Sometimes it is a result of a basic failure to accept the kind of commitment which marriage requires. And we might consider how much more shocking the divorce statistics would be if it were not for the large numbers of couples who do not bother to get married at all—and the dissolution of whose relationships are therefore never recorded.

Our society now manifests a host of social and personal problems which at first glance may seem not to have much to do with the family directly. Some of the most obvious include sexual promiscuity, pornography, homosexuality, drug use, alcoholism, vandalism, mental illness, and violence. If psychology and sociology have taught us anything, it is that pathologies of this kind are less likely to occur where family life is strong, and that where they do occur, they have probably been preceded by the breakdown of traditional family patterns.

Just what are the factors leading to the present level of family stress? The sexual revolution and certain aspects of the women's movement have had a tremendous impact upon traditional family relationships. The sexual revolution provided socially acceptable alternatives for gratification outside of marriage. The women's movement has substantially altered traditional roles within society. One result cited by many social scientists is a tremendous increase in the amount of friction within families. More and more women, many because of economic necessity, are now out of the home. Many of these are women who had been gaining a sense of self-esteem within the family unit, but who later turned to others outside the family in order to meet their needs. In too many instances, the end result has been divorce.

The current "do your own thing" trend has interfered with people's developing close and trusting family relationships. Often the emphasis is that people are neurotic if they feel a sense of responsibility for the feelings of other family members. People are also told to let all their feelings out, even if it is very hurtful to someone else.

Another problem is that family members do not talk and listen to each other as much as they used to. Children often say their parents are too busy to listen. People used to talk and listen at mealtime, but now many sit in front of the television sets with their dinners. Increased time spent watching TV and the consequent decrease in family communication have undoubtedly contributed to the weakening of family bonds.

While the women's liberation movement undoubtedly grew because of some genuine social inequities, a large part of the motivation behind that movement appears to be the desire to create a way of life which excludes the making of a home and the creation of a family. The negative impact of this movement on young women and on the family is enormous. The feminist movement is powerful and persuasive. Women who are making families are being told that they can find their true worth and ultimate fulfillment only by taking up a vocation or a profession. Many women heed this call, and their children, especially preschoolers, are the losers. Eventually society will be too. Many young women who have not married and who are struggling with unconscious conflicts having to do with feminine identity and heterosexual commitment are lured away from the making of a family. The making of a family may not be the role for every woman, but many young women would mature into satisfying family relationships if they were not lured away by the liberation movement.

Many women must take jobs because of economic need. Inflation is profoundly destructive to family life. After children are well launched into life, it makes good sense for a woman to resume finding challenges or developing talents outside the home if she so desires. Of course, unmarried women must support themselves. But consider this statistic: 54 percent of women with children who are teenagers and younger are working, and 39 percent of working women have preschool children. The absence of these women from home, particularly those with preschool children, will almost always have a negative impact of some degree on childhood development. Small babies need the continuous input of good mothering by one person. Some of the most severe damage to human development can be done to the human spirit when the child/mother bond is broken during the first three years of life.

When children are small and the mother is away most of the day, the quality of life in the home changes dramatically; only her presence can fill the void.

The cost of current family trends is enormous. Suicide is now the second highest cause of death of the young, and loneliness is a national symptom. These youngsters are too often lost and are filled with anguish. Finally, overcome by despair, they terminate the most precious gift of all—life itself. It is heartbreaking to observe the young who see what life has to offer but who cannot grab hold and make their own lives go forward. Loneliness is becoming a national illness. People are not just lonely because they are alone. They are lonely because they are empty inside, and that loneliness often comes from not having enjoyed good family life as children.

Drug usage among the young is not just a passing fad; it is an expression of the inner condition of the user. The user is seeking escape from pain caused by loneliness, from a life that fills him with anxiety and despair. The excited drug-induced state gives him courage. Other drugs lull consciousness. The end result is a poisoned human spirit which loses its effectiveness. A consistent finding in the life of the drug user is the absent father during the formative childhood years.

Drug usage in America is completely out of hand and will be a key element in our self-destruction. According to reliable surveys, 25 million Americans smoke marijuana regularly. The Presidential Commission on Mental Health estimates that 8 million American children need immediate help for psychiatric disorders; some estimates reach 30 million. In view of the disintegration in the durability of the male/female bond, the collapse of so many families, and the inability to make a complete bond by those who attempt it, that figure may be a mere drop in the bucket in the near future.

In view of the deterioration of family life and of the consequent displacement of children, it is no wonder that in one year 70,000 assaults were made on teachers, 100 murders were committed in schools, and a billion dollars' worth of property damage was done to schools. Many students in big cities are four to five years behind the level of achievement of children from smaller cities. These children are full of rage as a result of emotional deprivations and lack of authority within the home; they lack the inner controls to abide by external rules, by simple codes of human conduct. How can they be expected to behave in a civilized manner when they were deprived of civilizing experiences at home?

Venereal disease has reached an epidemic level. Approximately 10 million cases were reported during one year. Who knows how many cases were not reported! Realistic constraint on the sexual impulse is part of morality. To give in to one's impulses anytime, anywhere, and with anyone has become the "do your own thing" ethic of today. Epidemic venereal disease, along with millions of illegitimate babies, is part of the price that we are paying. One million children run away each year. Often these runaways are victims of sexual abuse. Cultures which do not place appropriate restraint on sexuality eventually decline.

The open display of pornography reflects this decline, as well as unrestrained sexual mores. Child pornography has become a multimillion-dollar business. Sad to say, millions of Americans enjoy looking at child pornography.

The prevalence of child abuse is skyrocketing. Small wonder, in light of the kind of family life many abusers experienced as children. It requires patience, generosity, tolerance, self-control, and the capacity to stand frustration to rear a child properly. Child abusers lack these qualities and were often physically abused themselves. They are passing on to their young what was done to them when they were young, and they also pass along the consequences of what was not done for them.

Overt homosexuality appears by most available measures to be on the increase, as might have been predicted. The causes of homosexuality are not completely known; but in some cases, homosexuality is traced to childhood experiences within the family and to the personalities of the parents and the nature of their relationship to the child. In some cases, homosexuality may be related to the faulty psychological development of the child, often within a disturbed family. It is an ominous fact, in my judgment, that the "gay movement" seeks to have its way of life redefined as a simple variant of normal human sexuality, a way of life woven into the fabric of society.

These are some of the sad facts of contemporary American life. These facts clearly reveal how much family life has changed in its structural makeup and value orientation.

However, despite all these difficulties, we dare not be

purveyors of doom and must continue to be hopeful. There is still a tremendous goodness in the people of America. Our young people have a generosity within them, and they are searching for the moral and spiritual values of life. Like many concerned people, I am not ready to acquiesce to forecasters of doom and hopelessness. Recent changes should not spell doom. They can be catalysts which encourage us to reexamine our attitudes about the family and to strengthen the basic foundations of family life.

It is so vitally important that you and I and our families and friends reaffirm very basic truths. The family, despite many and varied pressures, still gives life, and with prayer and effort on our part it will always remain the source of new life and love. The family will continue to offer a life-giving climate of security and stability in which individual persons can grow and thrive.

The family in American society enriches each of us with an identity from birth and really helps to make us all that we are or ever hope to be. There is no doubt that for most of us our family life influences a multitude of things that happen to us throughout life—for good or for bad.

Now when family life is being sorely tested and questioned, we must reinforce it as the primary stabilizer of our society. We must, to put it simply, return to our roots.

The family must be courageous, with every member willing to show to the world in a very tangible way the meaning of God's love for us and of our love for each other by praying and caring and sharing.

To be a family means to give service to those in need. We do this by being sensitive to each other's needs within the family and by reaching out and offering affirmation to one another. When we do this within the family, it very naturally follows that we reach out beyond the family to our neighbors in the community and even to suffering people in all parts of the world. We will work for justice and peace because of what we have learned and experienced in the family.

The family is the vital, lasting, and influential force in the life of all humanity. Strong, loving family relationships help us to face the problems and the challenges, the sorrows and the joys of life. Community, neighborhood, school, work, and personal friendships are important, but all, really, depend on the unique and powerful effects of the family.

The family is the primary institution of society. Through the family, positive basic human values are developed and handed on from one generation to another. The family is unmatched in its opportunity and responsibility to produce excellence. In essence, the family is still the best place for people to grow.

As the family goes, so goes our country and our society. The vitality, the creative energies, and the moral fiber of a culture are dependent on a stable family life. The conditions of our present, as well as our future, require the presence of men and women who have grown up within nurturing family environments. We must encourage an attitude in our local communities and in various levels of government which focuses on the importance of the family; and we must do all we can do to strengthen this most important of all our social institutions.

Our challenge is to proclaim clearly the intrinsic value of family life in our society.

The Value of
Family Life

Political and social planning in a wise social order begins with the axiom: *What strengthens the family strengthens society.* The family is the seedbed of economic skills, money habits, attitudes toward work, and the arts of financial independence. The family is a stronger agency of educational success than the school. The family is a stronger teacher of religious values than the church. If things go well with the family, life is worth living; when the family falters, life falls apart.

Much of contemporary wisdom tells us that putting another's needs and desires ahead of our own is foolish. But Paul reminds us, "God hath chosen the foolish things of the world to confound the wise" (1 Corinthians 1:27). Even the father who expends time, money, and energy on children when he could be living more luxuriously and "imaginatively" is often considered foolish in this world. How foolish to herself must the woman seem who chooses to forgo many of her own pleasures and to live, for a number of years at least, almost exclusively for others—unless her basic human impulses, which tell her that her conduct is right and good, are effectively reinforced? In my view, government, the media, churches, and other groups which influence our societal norms should provide such encouragement and support for this ethic if the moral foundations of our nation are to prevail.

There is not *one* family pattern in America—there are many. All are alike in this, however: They provide such civilization as exists in these United States with nurturing, grace, and hope—and they suffer greatly under the attacks of the media, of the economic system, and often of well-intentioned public programs.

Aggressive sentiments against marriage are usually expressed today in the name of "freedom," "openness," or "serious commitment to a career." Marriage is pictured as a form of imprisonment, oppression, boredom, and chafing hindrance. These accusations are not entirely without substance. But while marriage does indeed impose humbling and often frustrating responsibilities, these challenges are precisely the preconditions for true liberation. Marriage is not the enemy of moral development in adults. It is just the opposite.

A frightening statistic was pointed out in the September 1983 edition of *American Demographics*. Fully 59 percent of children born in 1983 will live with only one parent before they reach the age of eighteen, according to estimates by Arthur J. Norton, assistant chief of the Population Division of the Census Bureau, and an authority on household and family statistics. (See "Openers," p. 13.)

Children live in single-parent homes because they are born to unwed mothers, because their parents split up, or because a parent dies. Norton examined recent trends in premarital births and in divorce, separation, and death; he then applied current rates for these events to a hypothetical group of one hundred babies born in 1983.

Twelve of these hundred babies will be born to unwed mothers and will live with their mothers for at least one year. Forty more will be born to parents who will divorce before the children are eighteen. Five children will have parents who separate, and two will live in single-parent homes because one parent dies before the children are eighteen. Thus, a total of 59 percent will live with only one parent.

Norton's estimates imply that the single-parent home will be the norm for a majority of children sometime during their childhood.

One of the country's most respected sociologists, Dr. Amitai Etzioni of Columbia University, warned "that if we continue to dismember the American family at the present rate, we shall run out of families before we run out of oil." Etzioni further underscored the dramatic deterioration of the American family in recent years in the following statement: "If the number of married couples decreases at the accelerating rate it has over the past few years, the result will be no husband/wife families by the year 2008." (*Next*, May/June 1980, p. 28.) Although Dr. Etzioni surely does not seriously believe there will be no married couples in America by the turn of the century, to any thoughtful contemporary observer the tearing at the fabric of family life and the relationships of family members is self-evident.

Experts differ somewhat concerning the psychological effects of divorce on children, although most concur that the psychological impacts are generally adverse. A negative effect on children's economic well-being is almost inevitable. Before divorce, two parents and their children share one household, benefitting from economies of scale and from cooperative endeavors of the partnership. After divorce there are typically two households to maintain, the economies of scale are lost, and cooperative effort is more difficult, if not impossible.

Moreover, in most cases fathers provide little or no child support when the mother has custody. Fewer than half of such mothers receive child support payments from the father. Many divorced mothers must work full-time to support their children, and others depend partly or totally on government subsidy. Even so, more than 50 percent of the children in families headed by a female live in poverty, compared with only 8 percent in husband-wife families. (See Victor R. Fuchs, *New York Times,* 7 September 1983.)

I should like to suggest five reasons for society's interest in preserving such bedrock concepts as stable marriages.

First, family life meets the needs of children. Stability and continuity are so essential to child development that this factor alone justifies the legal preferences given to permanent kinship units.

Second, family life is the source of public virtue—a willingness to obey the unenforceable. It is through the commitments made in families that both children and parents experience the value of authority, responsibility, and duty in their most pristine forms. Those who formulated our constitutional system knew that public virtue among the citizenry was crucial to preserving the authority of popularly elected leaders.

The third reason for society's interest in the formal family is the family's role in preserving a democratic system of limited government. The immensely important responsibility of teaching values to children should be retained by the family and not allocated to government.

Fourth, formal marriage and family ties are essential to stability in our system of jurisprudence. A justifiable expectation that a relationship will continue indefinitely permits both society and the individuals involved to invest themselves in the relationship with a reasonable belief that the likelihood of future benefits warrants the risks and inconvenience of their personal investment.

The fifth reason is that reduction in national divorce rates will reduce the number of children living in poverty and decrease the size and cost of many government programs.

The assault on the family, particularly since the 1960s, together with growing economic stress, has given rise in families to a number of changes that earlier would have been considered deviant but are now simply referred to as "variant." Accompanying these drastic changes, however, have been warnings from many experts that there is no substitute for the family; and these same experts are predicting that if current social trends militating against families are not checked, the long-term social consequences will be disastrous. Many of these anti-family trends, including state-encouraged abortion, rampant pornography and obscenity, and aggressive homosexuality, are advocated by special interest groups whose self-interest is only too evident. America's public policy must be shifted to one which supports rather than denigrates families.

Existing and proposed public policies should be analyzed in terms of their impact upon families. Public policies should respect the sanctity of family life. Many tax policies and welfare laws, such as the requirement that a father must leave home for his family to receive assistance, should be carefully reviewed. Tax dollars spent to make sex counseling and prescription birth control drugs and devices available to minor children without cost and without the knowledge of parents violates the principle of parental responsibility for minor children. Millions of parents would deeply resent the violation of their right to know what is said and given to their children through government-supported entities.

Since the federal government became involved in funding these family planning and contraceptive programs, most researchers agree that virtually every problem the programs have sought to deter has become much worse:

- Teenage pregnancy rates have continued to rise, and the rate of teenage abortion has skyrocketed.
- Increasing millions are exposed to venereal disease and AIDS.
- Increasing numbers of illegitimate children are handicapped in their early lives as unwed mothers face the difficult task of raising their children alone.
- Public expenditures escalate as increasing numbers of single mothers join the welfare ranks, and we witness the increasing feminization of poverty in this country.

The "feminization of poverty" is not a future problem. It is a present, painful reality. Families headed by single women comprise the fastest growing segment of the poverty population.

We recognize that such tragic circumstances reflect a deeper societal problem of moral deterioration in our land. Government policies, however, should not aid and abet with taxpayers' dollars those programs which adversely affect the emotional and physical health of children, the values of families, and the rights and duties of parents.

In the Old Testament there are 23,214 verses. In the very last two of these verses the prophet Malachi seems to speak to our generation: "Behold, I will send you Elijah the prophet before the coming of the great and dreadful day of the Lord: and he shall turn the heart of the fathers to the children, and the heart of the children to their fathers, lest I come and smite the earth with a curse" (Malachi 4:5–6).

The values people live by are to a large extent a function of the quality of their family life and the training received when they were children. Healthy, mature, vital people embrace solid and constructive values, and society moves forward.

A better tomorrow begins with the training of a better generation. This places upon us as parents the responsibility to do more effective work in rearing and guiding our children. The home is the place where character is best formed and habits established. When parents recognize this role, the family and nation move forward—and when it is ignored, families and nations perish.

It is deplorable that a great nation like ours has watched marriages collapse on a scale quite unprecedented and has stood by with apparent indifference. Marriages and family in this country are going through a period of turbulent change and upheaval. Millions of men and women are going hopefully into marriage, struggling to succeed, giving up, getting divorced, parceling out their children, and marrying again—some succeeding the second time around, more failing again. Amid this scene of chaos and confusion, our national leadership in the main looks on, mostly indifferent, detached, usually uninvolved.

If we, the individual citizens, would speak out, the climate of public opinion could change. There is no need to denounce anyone—just to recognize that our family life is perhaps our most precious asset; that marriage can be a beautiful and fulfilling experience; that the responsible exercise of parenthood is a joyful task as well as a challenging human obligation. If we could keep hearing this kind of message and giving this kind of message, the cynics and detractors might realize that their abusive polemics are not well accepted. Then the youth of our land might begin to realize that men and women worthy of the greatest respect are in favor of marriage and in favor of families, leading to a change in their own attitudes and sense of personal responsibility.

On Becoming a
Better Father

In 1980 Dr. Urie Bronfenbrenner, then professor of psychology at Cornell University and one of our country's best known and most respected family researchers, spoke at a meeting of the National White House Conference on Families. His subject was "Who's Minding the Children?" His own answer to this question was: "Too often there is no competent, responsible adult to care."

As we know only too well, since that statement was made the number of "latchkey" children who come home to an empty house every day has been growing at dramatic rates. As we also know, such children contribute most heavily to rates of delinquency and other forms of aberrant behavior.

A child's most basic need, said Dr. Bronfenbrenner, is "the enduring and 'irrational' involvement of one or more adults in the child's life who share in joint activity with the child." Dr. Bronfenbrenner then explained that "irrational involvement" means the offering of love without conditions.

But the adult's "irrational involvement" must be a lasting, growing relationship as the shared activities become richer. Dr. Bronfenbrenner emphasized: "What we're talking about is a love affair that doesn't end—an adult who is totally committed to the child."

But the child's parent or caretaker can't just wait for love to happen spontaneously before he gets involved. In fact, said Bronfenbrenner, love must involve action first. Love is the emotional outcome of mutual involvement: the more an adult does with a child, the more the adult will love the child.

How effectively are children's needs being met? Not very effectively, most authorities agree. It's getting worse. Even parents who want to do a good job of parenting simply can't seem to find the time.

In our urban society more parents live on the freeway. An eight-to-five job often means leaving the house as early as 6:30 A.M. and getting home late. Not much of the day is left—and after the tension of the workday and of commuting, there's little desire for those precious hours of "joint activity" with the children.

More and more mothers are working, either by choice or because divorce, widowhood, or financial problems have forced them to be the breadwinners of their families. Naturally, there are fewer hours in the day for the children.

Just as dangerous is the attitude exacerbated in the last two decades, an attitude which has caused terrible damage: the motto "Do your own thing," which actually boils down to "Me first." Broken families and "broken" children are symptoms of that selfishness.

A society of people each of whom does his own thing is not a caring society. Such people do not make those desperately needed "irrational commitments" but instead look upon everything in life as disposable. Instead of deploring this uncaring society, many of us have come to accept this point of view; some say, "Marriage isn't working? Don't fix it—just get a new one." "Children are too demanding? Get a sitter."

There is no single public intervention program that can solve all the problems of America's children. Any solution must strike at the roots—and we need not wait for the government. People without professional training are often the people with the real power to make those needed changes in children's lives.

There is no way parents can evade having a determining effect upon their children's personalities, character, and competence. Dr. Diana Baumrind, a research psychologist from the Institute of Human Development at the University of California at Berkeley, says, "Children are not able to alter their own environment the way adults can—and so whether parents mean to or not, they have a profound controlling influence on their children's lives."

Dr. Baumrind worked with a large group of children and their parents, studying what kind of parenting is associated with different behavior patterns in the children. Her findings indicate that there are three basic kinds of parents: authoritarian, permissive, and authoritative.

Authoritarian parents value obedience as a virtue in itself. They work at keeping the child subordinate, preserving order as an end in itself rather than as a means of accomplishing other purposes. Their method is rigorous discipline, either physical or emotional (shaming, for example).

Permissive parents, on the contrary, view themselves as a resource for the child. They do not try to control the child or get him to obey. Rather, they keep the child free from restraint and let him grow as he wants.

Dr. Baumrind explained that the type of parenting she has found most effective lies somewhere between these two extremes; it is what she calls authoritative parenting. To authoritative parents, obedience is a means of promoting learning. Authoritative parents reason with their children, explaining why a certain rule is necessary, why a certain punishment must be imposed. At the same time, the child's wishes and desires are respected. Standards for behavior are set, but the child is free within those standards to choose what he wants, and the rules are never arbitrarily or whimsically chosen.

Being a parent is perhaps the most influential role most of us will ever have. Yet too often parenthood means exclusively "motherhood." Mothers are vital to the happiness and well-being of the family, but the influence of a good father can be just as valuable. Professional research has found that a child's intellectual, emotional, and social development, his or her masculinity and femininity, and even the ability to function effectively in a future marriage appear to be influenced by the father's personal relationship with the child and with the child's mother.

Over two thousand children of all ages and backgrounds were asked why they appreciated their fathers. "He takes time for me" was the essence of their replies.

If fathers were to add up the time actually spent with their children, the total may not be as much as they might think. In one study of three-month-old infants, it was found that fathers spent only thirty-eight seconds a day with their young children! When a father doesn't give sufficient time to a child, not only is that child deprived of a father's important positive influence but in some instances the child may even be harmed. Evidence has shown that a child who is always shunned or ignored will begin to think of himself as worthless. Giving time to your children, the kind of time that will help them feel good about themselves, about life, and about others—including you—is the first major step in becoming a better father.

Because time is so crucial, many time-related problems can arise in father-child relationships, including:

- Lack of time. Fathers never seem to have enough time. Most work long hours and are constantly involved in business, church, athletics, and civic responsibilities. Home becomes a stopping place between other obligations. Often the few conversations we have with our children center around the theme "I'm busy."
- Preoccupation with other matters. Many fathers give time to their children but are so preoccupied with their own thoughts or activities that they may as well not even be there. Too often we watch the game on TV while reading children a bedtime story. We think about how we're going to fix the car while helping a child with some homework. Often we are physically present, but mentally and emotionally absent.
- Frustration. Too often, also, when we give time to our children we may feel that it is a burden. We may take them to the zoo but wish we hadn't. Perhaps we think of the time being taken away from something else we'd rather be doing.

Almost every father, on occasion, becomes too busy, too preoccupied, or too frustrated to relate well with his children. The danger occurs when these problems arise frequently or in ways that become harmful to children.

Children are our most important assets. They need our time. Once we understand the importance of our influence on our children and correct our priorities, there are several steps we should consider.

Pay attention. You pay attention to your child by responding to his presence, particularly when he is speaking. Paying attention means looking at the child instead of the newspaper or television set, listening carefully to feelings as well as words, asking him for an opinion about what you're discussing, showing genuine interest instead of annoyance. Just as much is said with facial expressions and the tone of voice as with words. Let your actions tell your children you're paying attention.

Share your experiences. Sharing takes place when you and your child talk and listen. It happens when you exchange ideas, experiences, and concerns; interests and ambitions; likes and dislikes. While there are personal and intimate experiences which should not be shared, most fathers could be much more open with their children.

Do things with your children. A child needs to enjoy family activities and traditions. But he also needs moments when he can be alone with his father on a one-to-one basis. Participating in planned activities (such as camping, building a tree house, going to the museum or library) as well as enjoying spur-of-the-moment activities (such as going for a walk, working in the yard, going to the store together) are important ways to spend time with your child.

Doing things together is especially significant to the

child if the activity is something he or she wants to do. But the activity is secondary. What's important is that you're there, focusing all your time and attention on the child. That means being involved in activities with your daughter as well as with your son.

Make "later" now. Fathers often have a "later" attitude toward their children. "I'll help you later. I'm busy now." Or, "Don't bother me now. Maybe later." The challenge as a father is to make "later" now. Start right now to take those precious moments of time to respond to the needs of your children in positive ways. Your children will grow up, but they'll never outgrow the need to spend time with their father.

The role of the family—a father, a mother, and children who respect them—is the critical center of social force. As we are prone to quote within the Church, "No other success can compensate for failure in the home."

CHAPTER TEN

A Prescription for Healthy Families

My observations concerning the severe problems facing contemporary families derive from an adult lifetime of firsthand experience and observation. Besides a bit of "cursing the darkness" that currently exists on the American family scene, I hope to light some candles by offering some positive, practical suggestions for improving healthy functioning of the families to which we belong.

As mentioned earlier, the family is rapidly deteriorating with serious economic and psychological and social consequences. Families are falling apart, and single-parent families are becoming more common each year.

In a 1983 article in *U.S. News and World Report*, psychologist David Elkind is quoted as follows: "The rise of single parenthood is a serious development, because it leaves an enormous segment of our population with less defense against the dangerous stresses of daily living" (in James Mann, "One-Parent Family: The Troubles— and the Joys," *U.S. News and World Report,* 28 November 1983, p. 57).

Later in that same 1983 article are found the following statements:

Those wondering how children fare in one-parent households can draw on a growing body of professional advice and evidence, much of it discouraging. Sociologist Amitai Etzioni, University Professor at George Washington University in Washington, D.C., declares: "In all my professional and personal experience, I have not seen a single child who did not suffer to some degree, physically or psychosomatically, from divorce."

One place handicaps surface is in school, where a study for the National Institute of Education shows that children living with only one parent average as much as 7 points lower than their classmates in IQ and several months behind on achievement tests. Higher dropout rates also are common.

The authors of the report explain: "Children in divorced and other one-parent families tend to be more disruptive in the classroom, have less-efficient work or study habits and tend to be absent, truant or tardy more often. These behaviors may interfere with application of knowledge as evidenced in poorer quality of classroom work."

Studies also show that juvenile-delinquency rates are twice as high for youngsters from single-parent homes as for those in traditional households. Although children raised by one parent comprise just over a fifth of their age group, they commit 55 percent of its crimes, reports the Behavioral Research Institute in Boulder, Colorado. "Clearly, single-parent families are a significant factor in the causes of juvenile crime," says the institute's director, Delbert Elliott. (Mann, "One-Parent Family," pp. 58, 62.)

In the face of the rampant and well-publicized social indicators pointing up the pathology of the American family, what are some of the practical, time-tested recommendations for making our families what God intended and what we so want them to be? Author Dolores Curran conducted a survey among five hundred professionals whose jobs require them to work closely with families. From that survey she formed a list of the top fifteen traits of a healthy family, and presented them in her book *Traits of a Healthy Family* as follows:

The healthy family . . .

1. communicates and listens.
2. affirms and supports one another.
3. teaches respect for others.
4. develops a sense of trust.
5. has a sense of play and humor.
6. exhibits a sense of shared responsibility.
7. teaches a sense of right and wrong.
8. has a strong sense of family in which rituals and traditions abound.
9. has a balance of interaction among members.
10. has a shared religious core.
11. respects the privacy of one another.
12. values service to others.
13. fosters family table time and conversation.

14. shares leisure time.
15. admits to and seeks help with problems.
(From *Traits of a Healthy Family* [Minneapolis, Minn.: Winston Press, 1983], pp. 23–24.)

From a dear friend and colleague, Richard W. Linford —an attorney, active member of the Church, father of eight, devoted husband, and practical counselor—I have the following list of "Twenty Ways to Make a Good Marriage Great":

1. *Night and morning prayer*—to say thanks, to ask for help in your marriage and family, to worship together.
2. *A weekly planning meeting*—to discuss the calendar, talk over needs and problems, decide priorities and next steps. (Write decisions in a journal, including goals and discussion topics, and reasons for each.)
3. *A daily phone call or personal conversation*—to say "I love you," to touch base, to discuss the day, to show you care.
4. *A weekly date*—to a favorite park, a concert, the library, the gym; or staying home for a candlelight dinner, a game, or a mutual hobby.
5. *Patience regardless*—of missed meals, tardiness, forgotten favors, a thoughtless remark, impatience.
6. *Daily service*—helping with house or yard work, mending a piece of clothing, taking a turn with the sick baby, fixing a favorite meal. (Write it down. Do it!)
7. *A budget*—to tie down income and expenses, help set financial goals, and give you control over your finances.

8. *Listening*—not only to what is said, but also to what is meant.
9. *Regular attendance*—at church, and where possible, the temple.
10. *Daily scripture reading*—to learn the gospel, to receive inspiration for yourself and your marriage, to become more like Jesus.
11. *Working together*—caring for a garden, painting a bedroom, washing the car, scrubbing floors, building a piece of furniture, writing a poem together, team teaching a class.
12. *Forgiving each other daily*—always learning from each other, trying a different way, being the first to make peace.
13. *Courtesies*—like saying please and thank you, not interrupting or belittling, not doing all the talking, continuing the niceties of courtship.
14. *Soft and kind words*—of tenderness, compassion, empathy.
15. *Learning together by*—reading to each other, discussing ideas, taking a class.
16. *Respecting*—opinions, ideas, privacy.
17. *Supporting your spouse's*—Church callings and righteous goals.
18. *Caring for your spouse's family by*—enjoying their company, praying for them, serving them, overlooking differences.
19. *Occasional gifts*—such as a note, a needed item, but mostly gifts of *time* and *self.*
20. *Loving with all your heart*—"Thou shalt love thy wife [thy husband] with all thy heart, and shalt cleave unto her [him] and none else" (D&C 42:22). (*Ensign*, December 1983, pp. 64-65.)

More than forty years of happy married life have convinced me of the efficacy of this formula. I have learned, however, that after all is said and done, more is usually *said* than *done*. These simple steps, thoughtfully and consistently pursued, will provide a tremendous lift to the quality of marriage and family life. And building a strong family is a goal well worth all the work and sacrifice involved.

PART THREE _____

Youth

_____

The Lifelong Quest for Truth

I love the youth of the Church, and I would like to address the remarks in this chapter directly to the youth. Though there are differences between my generation and yours, there are similarities too.

Both my generation and yours, separated by three or four decades of living, are searching for answers, trying to discover, anxious to uncover or to reveal truth. This universal urge is fostered and kept alive by a discontent which abides within us. We are all, in other words, on a lifelong quest for truth, ever pursuing but never completely arriving.

The spirit of adventure—the desire to know, to explore, to discover what is on the other side of the mountain, in the ocean, or in outer space—is age-old and worldwide.

Surely no generation was ever so well equipped or so prepared to continue the quest as is yours. The searching spirit is part of your inheritance. Keep it alive and active.

I hope that as you go through life your souls will carry a question mark as an indelible brand, that the spirit of intelligent inquiry will continue to gnaw at you as long as life lasts. An old proverb expresses this spirit of eager inquiry: "Age is wise, it attempts nothing impossible; youth is wiser, it believes nothing impossible."

My appeal to you who are entering upon the journey of life is that you build solidly and confidently upon the foundations laid by your predecessors, foundations which are deep and broad enough to support whatever superstructure your genius may enable you to build. Continue to seek for answers to ever-multiplying questions.

I counsel you to appreciate your parents, whose desire is to help you learn. In your relationships with them, let your hearts be increasingly turned to each other, and let your words of affection and appreciation touch each other.

It is also important while you are still young that you decide who you really are as children of God, what you want to be, where you want to go, and the price you are willing to pay to get there.

Your generation possesses powers conferred by science to wreck or rebuild the world, and the degree to which you carry faith in God, in your fellowman, and in yourselves will determine whether these tremendous forces be used to build a better world or be responsible for its destruction.

Leading scientists are urgently calling attention to the need for peace, for brotherhood, and for mutual understanding if our civilization is to survive. We must have peace or we might have nothing.

We can achieve this most desirable goal if we wisely use the two most potent forces in civilization—religion and science. True religion will help us to minimize the evils of envy, greed, intolerance, and lust for power, while science will reduce the physical burdens of mankind and make the earth more fruitful. We can create plenty in place of scarcity, break down the barriers of ignorance and misunderstanding, and make life more desirable, more meaningful, and more fruitful for everyone. But the current cynicism and materialism must be resisted and replaced by spiritual vitality.

In spite of these sobering challenges, may I suggest the need for a sense of humor. Dr. Lowell L. Bennion once advised a son of mine as he set forth on a challenging missionary assignment halfway around the world. Instead of profound and erudite counsel, he simply said, "Gordon, just remember to laugh a little each day."

A sense of humor is needed in order to preserve your sanity during your college days, when you contend with the strange behavior of your professors. You will need it again when you marry and are mystified by the mysteries of the opposite sex. Abraham Lincoln is reported to have said, "If I could not tell or hear a good story occasionally, I think I should go crazy. It is like oxygen to my soul." Elder J. Golden Kimball on one occasion said, "I think God himself must like a joke; if he hadn't, he would not have made some of you people."

I hope that you will gain from your formal education a greater appreciation of and appetite for good books. Comparatively few American adults now read out of the best books. Instead, indiscriminate watching of television has become the national pastime. Unfortunately, heavy watchers of television often tend to become spectators at almost everything else, and republics and democracies do not flourish with spectator citizens. I urge you to learn to enjoy reading.

I encourage you to think in terms of some sort of formal education beyond high school. So much of your later life will depend upon the thoroughness with which you are educated and prepared in your youth. Don't sell yourselves short in what you will eventually accomplish academically.

As one who has spent nearly twenty years in some form of college-related training I can attest to the enrichment which continuing education can offer. My own formal education taught me how much I did not yet know and also how subdivided and specialized knowledge is — a pretty good argument for the need for continuing education.

Hopefully, you will also gain from your educational experiences the skill to differentiate between mere information and wisdom. Popular phrases like "knowledge explosion" and "information revolution," when not used precisely and thoughtfully, ignore the stark reality that there is no democracy among facts: Not all facts are of equal significance!

Pay no attention to the pompous pessimists who predict our downfall, who constantly magnify the strength and ability of the enemy and minimize our own. Avoid extremism and hysteria in all forms and be guided by levelheaded common sense.

While the two terms *learning* and *education* are frequently used as if they were synonymous, you know already that mere learning may have but little to do with real education. A person may know Latin, Greek, mathematics, music, art, and literature, and still be totally unable to cope with the problems that may arise in his life. If you become a slave to habits and are unable to master yourselves, you may be classified as being learned but certainly not educated.

On the other hand, a man may be absolute master of himself and of his environment and may develop his faculties and powers so as to deal wisely with the problems of life, and still know little of Latin and Greek, the arts and the sciences.

Beware of overspecialization. We must not allow specialized training to destroy God-given individuality or to standardize our activities and our lives until we become mere automated robots.

I should like to briefly discuss two kinds of education:

The first comes from classes in school and from our teachers, and the second comes from life itself and from the necessity of earning one's living. When we combine the two types, the result is magnificent. Such a student learns to reason, to recognize truth, to love beauty, and to hate evil.

Real and worthwhile and usable education is more than merely guided growth. It has its springs within the soul of man and is concerned with life itself. Education should lay a foundation for life and train man to make an honest living, to have convictions, and to stand for truth and right without flinching, whether or not it may be fashionable or popular to do so.

The kind of education which we are discussing teaches the dignity of honest labor and should make it possible for each of us to find and do the work for which he or she is best fitted. Good education also convinces us that all knowledge is hurtful if it lacks goodness.

The truly educated person is receptive to new ideas, is free from prejudice, and has the ability to distinguish between appearance and reality. Ralph Waldo Emerson wrote, "It is easy in the world to live after the world's opinion; it is easy in solitude to live after our own, but the great man is he who in the midst of a crowd keeps with perfect sweetness the independence of solitude."

Education enables one to apply a cultivated mind to the problems of living. It provides trained judgment and makes for ability to discriminate, freedom, and tolerance to understand the point of view of others and to give to others' viewpoints the freedom which one demands for one's own. Thus a person will be able to live with his fellowmen in harmony and cooperate in promoting good will. Upon the educated people of the country depends the progress of civilization.

The one great gift of education is that it gives us the ambition to dream, to do, to become, each according to his talents. It gives us the will to continue in the struggle, no matter how great the odds against us. We must care enough about the future of the world never to be satisfied with the present.

All lasting wealth is of the heart. The things that really gratify are things that money cannot buy. A man or a nation may be comparatively rich in material comforts and yet very poor in moral, intellectual, and spiritual endowments.

Some few of you may actually make your way to the nation's or world's centers of economic and political power. However, most of you will not. You will enrich the world, but without shaping it dramatically or in its entirety.

However, most of you will be parents. All of you will be neighbors. All of you will be citizens, whether in Fayette or Philadelphia, Manti or Miami. For the great majority of you, the most important work you will do will be within the walls of your own homes.

I cannot promise you an easy life, nor would I secure it for you if I could, for man's life is similar to the life of a tree whose roots are driven down into the solid earth by the winds and storms which will either strengthen or destroy it. As Douglas Malloch wrote:

> Good timber does not grow in ease;
> The stronger wind, the stronger trees;
> The further sky, the greater length,
> The more the storm, the more the strength.
> By sun and cold, by rain and snow,
> In tree or man good timbers grow.

You will need determination, endurance, self-discipline, knowledge, and love of God and of fellowmen. With it all you must muster the courage, in Kipling's words, to "hold on when there is nothing in you except the will that says to you, 'Hold on!' "

The following poem was prepared by Henry Wadsworth Longfellow and read on the fiftieth anniversary of his school's graduating class. He titled it "Morituri Salutamus." This was the gladiators' cry in the arena as they stood face to face with death. Longfellow left this message to the young men of his time, and perhaps it is appropriate in modern times too.

> And ye who fill the places we once filled,
> And follow in the furrow that we tilled,
> Young friends, whose generous hearts are beating high,
> We who are old, and are about to die,
> Salute you; hail you; take your hands in ours,
> And crown you with our welcome as with flowers!
> How beautiful is youth! How bright it gleams
> With its illusions, aspirations, dreams!
>
> What shall I say to you? What can I say
> Better than silence is? When I survey

This throng of faces turned to meet my own
Friendly and fair, and yet to me unknown.
. . . .
The unwritten only still belongs to thee;
Take heed, and ponder well what that shall be.

I counsel you that if you wish to enjoy this great
journey of life to its fullest, follow the pattern given in
the scriptures: "Seek ye first the kingdom of God and
his righteousness, and all these things shall be added
unto you" (3 Nephi 13:33).

May God bless, guide, and accompany you on your
journey and then at last welcome you joyously with,
"Well done, thou good and faithful servant."

_____

CHAPTER TWELVE

Setting
Goals

_____

When I was called to be a bishop, I was counseled by our general Church leadership that my greatest responsibility was to provide spiritual guidance and direction to the young people of our nearly thousand-member ward congregation. In the ensuing years, from this age group would come some of my experiences of deepest concern and of greatest heartache, and some of my most satisfying moments.

I participated in hundreds of personal interviews, numerous youth trips, countless priesthood, Scouting, and Young Women's programs, and scores of meetings in which young people spoke of their faith in God and in his Son, our Savior. These experiences reinforced my faith and confidence in the choice young people of that generation. Notwithstanding this faith and confidence in that generation and in the present one, I have come to believe in the need for a greater sense of direction for most youth of the Lord's Church—the need to be motivated, to set and achieve appropriate spiritual and temporal goals in life.

I recall an occasion when, as I approached a freeway entrance on my way out of Salt Lake City, I observed three young people, at intervals of perhaps a hundred yards, standing at the side of the highway. Each carried a sign indicating a destination city he hoped to achieve with the assistance of a willing motorist. The first sign indicated Los Angeles, the second, San Francisco. The last, in larger letters than the others, was a sign which said simply, "Anywhere."

This sign seemed to me symbolic of the dilemma and frustration faced by so many young people who seemingly lack a sense of direction for their lives and who don't really know what their destination should be. A thoughtful adult advised me in my teen years that the world would get out of the way for a young person who knew where he or she was going. I vividly recall an eighth grade class in which a wise teacher attempted to stimulate and encourage the students in his class with a vision of future life goals. He asked each student to state a professional or vocational lifetime goal. My own response was that I wanted to be a farmer and a teacher. The teacher responded, "That sounds pretty good, but if you are going to be a teacher you should have another job so you can make a living." One of my classmates received considerable good-natured heckling from the rest of us when he said, "I plan to become a physician." In our quiet rural community, such a goal appeared beyond the reach of any thirteen-year-old boy.

I watched this young man over the next ten or more

years as he pursued a steady course towards his stated professional goal. Despite the interruption of World War II and the challenge of being a member of a large family with limited economic means, he stayed on his course. Three decades later, I met this former classmate in a distant city. I reminded him of the impression his clearly stated life goal had made upon my youthful mind. His response was characteristic of his attitude and parental training: "Without a clear goal, I could never have accomplished my objective and risen above the obstructions that were in my path."

As a young bishop those many years ago, I became convinced that setting clear and realistic goals was crucial to the spiritual and temporal success of the youth of our ward. Many of these young people came from homes where inadequate thought and direction were given to encourage young minds and hearts to set and achieve worthwhile goals for their lives. This choice group of young people was beset on every side, as today's youth are, by worldly, distracting influences, and by a prevailing attitude of "just getting by." Clearly, young people cannot rise from obscurity and darkness to fulfill their promised potential and destiny if apathy and indulgence are their daily fare.

As adult leaders, we prayerfully approached the task of trying to help the large group of choice young people rise to higher ground. We felt the responsibility to help them set and achieve gospel-centered goals in their lives. Many young people then—and I believe even more so now—without strong personal commitment and inspired parental and Church leadership are destined to live lives far below that abundant life promised by the Savior. In seminary many years earlier I had learned this verse:

To every man there openeth
A Way, and Ways, and a Way.
And the High Soul climbs the High Way,
And the Low Soul gropes the Low,
And in between, on the misty flats,
The rest drift to and fro.
But to every man there openeth
A High Way, and a Low.
And every man decideth
The way his soul shall go."

(John Oxenham)

One part of our plan to encourage these youth was what I called a "do-it-yourself life prediction experiment." This experiment first involved the teenaged young men of our ward and later the young women. On a Sunday morning in early January 1960, we met in a special meeting with approximately fifty youth of our ward. The timing of the meeting proved an interesting coincidence. The very week of our meeting was to usher in the tumultuous period of the 60s,—a decade often described as the time of the greatest youth rebellion and domestic strife and turbulence in the history of our nation. It was to be the decade of assassinations of some of our nation's top leaders, the Vietnam War, riots and looting, the Beatles, Woodstock, and in some of our nation's cities a virtual breakdown in our ability to govern ourselves.

All fifty of the youth attending this meeting agreed to participate in an exercise of foretelling the future. Each person was given a pencil and a blank sheet of lined paper. The group ranged in age from twelve to nineteen years, with nearly equal distribution of each age level. Together we concluded that many of the most crucial and fundamental decisions in each person's future would take place during the next ten years.

We next determined by joint discussion those questions of greatest importance to the members of the group —questions which the next ten years would in large measure answer. After a period of deliberation, the following questions were determined to be of greatest personal interest to those members of the group participating:

1. What kind of education will I receive?
2. What will be my life's work and occupation?
3. Will I be married?
4. Will I be active in the Church and be living the gospel's teachings?
5. Will I fill a mission?
6. Where will I be living?

In later years I involved other groups of youth in similar exercises. With minor variations I found that the same interests and concerns for the future were expressed by most of the young people in the Church when similarly questioned.

After determining the questions listed above, we emphasized to those young people back in 1960 that within certain obvious limits, many of these critical questions bearing on their future happiness and accomplishment were within their own capacity to determine or at least strongly influence the outcome.

After we reached consensus on the questions of greatest concern, each person was then asked to write his own answer or prediction to each question. We promised the youth that their answers would be completely confidential and known only to themselves.

Their answers were then placed in a sealed envelope. I agreed to maintain the envelope in a confidential file for a period of ten years.

As part of our pact with the young people, we adult leaders agreed to contact all members attending that January 1960 meeting for the follow-up part of the experiment ten years later in January 1970. As a bishopric we agreed to host a turkey dinner for these youth and their companions if they were married. In ten years the envelope would be opened and each paper would be returned to its owner. Each might then determine how well his life to that point had fulfilled his own written ten-year goal predictions.

The decade of the turbulent sixties rolled on. Life was full of change and adjustment, both for the young people and their Church leaders. During the next ten years, a majority of those attending the January 1960 meeting completed successful missions, and a majority by 1970 had married.

I don't mean to overemphasize the significance of this experiment in the lives of these young poeple. Their later decisions and accomplishments represented the currents of many forces and events perhaps too complex to properly assess. Greatest of all the influences were undoubtedly those which took place within the walls of the young people's own homes. Nevertheless, this experiment provided an excellent opportunity, in later visits and personal interviews with each young person, for me to ask, "How are you coming with your goals?" In later years, many of these young folks reminded their Church leaders of this earlier goal-setting exercise. As adult Church leaders and friends we attempted to keep fresh in the minds of the participants the future personal self-assessment which was to follow a few short years hence.

During the intervening ten-year period, we emphasized the need for these youth to set short-range and intermediate-range goals. We cited the relationship of these short-term goals to those long-range objectives earlier mentioned in the experiment. The relationship between long-term goals and short-range activities often seems difficult for many to comprehend. For example: the importance of adequate personal study and commitment today to achieve long-time academic goals in the future; the requirement of obedience, faithful Church activity and gospel study to prepare for useful, mature Church service; the need to *do* the will of Heavenly Father if we are to know of the gospel's truthfulness— such relationships are something that perhaps we all need to better understand.

For those of us who were the adult leaders in the 1960 meeting, the next ten years passed quickly. Many of us by 1970 held other Church assignments. Our obligation, however, to reconvene this group of youth now grown to maturity was still firmly fixed in our minds. A faithful former associate prepared a list of currently available addresses of all who had attended the earlier 1960 meeting. Our wives prepared the promised turkey dinner. Some of the group were then serving in the military in Southeast Asia. One of these, who had also earlier served a successful Church mission, was represented by his wife, now the mother of their two beautiful sons. (I might add that this young man eventually served as a bishop, became the father of five more children, and has come to know the joys of being a busy grandfather.)

The dinner proceeded with great warmth and fellowship. Many of those attending had not seen each other for years. Spirited tales of "remember when" brought nostalgic memories of earlier choice youthful associations and experiences. Personal testimonies emphasized the importance and blessings of the gospel in the lives of these young people now grown to maturity, most with families of their own.

Finally, the long-preserved sealed envelope was opened. Each person attending received his original self-completed ten-year prediction sheet. Some shared their earlier predictions with enthusiasm and humor. Others had forgotten both the original questions and the answers they had given to those questions. For many, however, opening the envelope was very meaningful. Their Church, education, marriage, and career goals had been thoughtfully stated. They had remembered and determinedly pursued these goals in the ten years that had intervened. Many of these youth of an earlier period with young hopes and dreams were now adults of considerable accomplishment.

It would provide a happy ending if I could report that all those of the earlier decade were present and accounted for in this dinner meeting. I believe I still have the self-prediction sheets of a small number of the youth who did not attend the later meeting. In scriptural language, a few had at that stage of life "fallen by the wayside."

Their current life-style was no longer gospel-centered. Some were casualties to the cunning attractions of him who would pervert the Savior's great plan and purpose for us all. He who would lead us all from the Lord's path had been successful in making his counterfeit forms of joy—amounting to nothing more than worldly indulgence—at least temporarily more attractive to a few of these young people, whose places at the table were empty on this otherwise pleasant and uplifting occasion. Our desire had been that all the original participants would attend. A few in the original group no longer shared common interests and goals with the majority who did attend. As their Church leaders of an earlier day we asked ourselves, "With a bit more effort and concern on our part, could their lives perhaps have been touched for good and their paths made more straight?"

It is my hope that parents and adult leaders will love and lift today's choice generation of youth to higher ground that they might realize the great promise of Paul to the Corinthians: "Eye hath not seen, nor ear heard, neither have entered into the heart of man, the things which God hath prepared for them that love him" (1 Corinthians 2:9). If parents and leaders will make every effort possible to guide the youth toward obtaining such divine rewards, and if the youth will work diligently toward achieving their potential and reaching their righteous goals in life, all of them will find these blessings of happiness and fulfillment realized in their lives.

Patriarchal Blessings
Build Strength

As we consider sources of strength that the youth of the Church can rely on, we should be mindful of the great source of faith and direction to be found in patriarchal blessings. From firsthand experience I have come to appreciate the great inspiration and stability to our lives that a patriarchal blessing can provide. Mine has been a compass and a constant guiding star to me ever since I received it. I received my patriarchal blessing from a family patriarch, Brother Israel Bennion, my father's cousin, under rather unusual circumstances.

My father had served virtually all his married life as the bishop of our pioneer ward in the Taylorsville, Utah, area. He and my mother were the parents of six young children, ages four to fourteen, when my father was stricken with pneumonia in January 1932 and died suddenly. My oldest brother, who was fourteen years old, died just ten days later from an unrelated illness.

My grief-stricken mother was left bereft to raise the five remaining children and to act as both father and mother. The period marked the depths of the Great Depression. Times were difficult for everyone. My mother had been a registered nurse before her marriage, and after a period of time she was able to return to nursing in order to help provide for her remaining children. She was able to raise them and help them fulfill Church missions and pursue educational goals.

A year after my father's passing, Patriarch Israel Bennion came to our home and gave each of mother's living children a patriarchal blessing. I still have a vivid memory of each child according to age being given his or her blessing in the dining room of our family home. The impression of this event on my youthful mind was singular. I believed then as I believe now that those blessings were prophetic and given by the inspiration of Almighty God.

My own blessing totaled only 263 words. Each word of that blessing has become more precious to me as the years have passed. Two promises in the blessing have been especially prophetic in my life. One extract is as follows: "You shall be called to positions of trust, even to be a 'judge in Israel.' " To a child of seven years of age, the title *judge in Israel* seemed much too profound a term to understand. In later teenage years, however, I learned that to be a judge in Israel was to be a bishop. I carried my patriarchal blessing with me during military service in World War II. Somehow that promise and others contained in the blessing gave me hope and faith that I would survive the conflict and live to perform other service in our Heavenly Father's kingdom.

When I was called to be a bishop as a young father at

age thirty-one I reflected again on the literal fulfillment of that earlier promise to me, which patriarchal promise was clearly not known to those who called me to that position. For the next seven years I came to know the true joy of being a "judge in Israel."

Another promise contained in the blessing that I have lived to see literally fulfilled is the following: "You shall see great progress in the work of the Lord, for Zion shall be the head and not the heel." This phrase has repeatedly come to my mind in recent years as I have observed the growth and progress of the Lord's church and have been able to meet with Latter-day Saints in many places of the world, including Eastern Europe, Hispanic America, and even the People's Republic of China.

Especially memorable to me, as literal fulfillment of this blessing, was a meeting at the Church Administration Building in 1984 during which President Gordon B. Hinckley, representing the Church's First Presidency, all the members of the Council of the Twelve, and the presidents of the women's organizations of the Church were visited by President Ronald Reagan, then the president of the United States. The next day the same group met with his opponent for the presidency, former Vicepresident Walter Mondale. A photo of that memorable meeting with the president of the United States shows President Hinckley reading to President Reagan from Ether 2:9 in the Book of Mormon: "And now, we can behold the decrees of God concerning this land, that it is a land of promise; and whatsoever nation shall possess it shall serve God, or they shall be swept off when the fulness of his wrath shall come upon them."

From these and many other experiences I have come to know the blessing and the personal prophecy to us that are contained in our patriarchal blessings. In these challenging times when the youth of the Church are growing to maturity and are faced with great temptations and often compromising peer group pressure, patriarchal blessings can be a source of great strength and can instill faith in a loving, personal Heavenly Father.

PART FOUR _____

Spirit

Latter-day Pioneers

It is good to pause and reflect on those courageous souls of years past who prepared the way for us to live the blessed lives we now enjoy. The blessings they have bequeathed us we sometimes accept all too passively, not fully aware of how they have touched our lives in very direct ways.

Many of our forebears came from other nations, leaving us the legacy of freedom, opportunity, and education. Some have passed down to us the gifts of music, dance, art, or literature, gifts that shape our appreciation for our lives on this earth and enrich our enjoyment of it. Some of them left their homes and families to gather to Zion, and they left us an unmatched heritage too.

Many of us have ancestors who came across the plains with the Mormon pioneers. Though we may not all have blood ties with these early pioneers, they are spiritual forebears to all of us in the Church. We all reap benefits from their courageous pioneer spirit.

They were not the only pioneers this land has seen. The pioneer spirit has swept over this land many times and continues to do so. That spirit is grounded in faith, in courage, in dreaming dreams, in taking the risk of venturing into unknown territory. It is prompted by something within each of us that whispers to us we should be prepared to devote our lives to that in which we believe.

Let me review some facts pertaining to those first few days when the pioneers of 1847 came into the Salt Lake Valley. On July 24, before eating his dinner, Wilford Woodruff, who entered the valley along with Brigham Young, planted the one-half bushel of potatoes he had brought across the plains. He hoped, by the blessings of the Lord, to save enough for seed the following year. There were no idlers in the camp. They were as busy as they possibly could be looking to the future.

It was the general opinion among the pioneers who came in 1847 that it never rained in the Salt Lake Valley during the summer season. Somehow or other they had heard that and believed it. However, on the evening of July 24 there was a beautiful thundershower, and it rained for a short time over the entire valley. This came as a special blessing to the people and gave them hope that their crops would survive.

It was just four days after their arrival that Brigham Young and the members of the Quorum of the Twelve Apostles who were in the valley met together and selected the spot where the temple was to be erected. They designated the ten-acre block, which we now call Temple Square, to be the center place of the city.

Another interesting thing is that on July 29, just five days after Brigham Young arrived, a large group of one hundred forty members of the Mormon Battalion marched into the city. They had just finished their assignments for the United States government and came to join the rest of the body. They brought with them a hundred Church converts from Mississippi, who had been with them in a camp near Pueblo, Colorado. This large group that joined the others brought with them sixty wagons, one hundred head of horses and mules, and three hundred head of cattle, all of which served to strengthen materially the settlement of the initial pioneers.

While some were exploring, others were plowing and planting; so in less than one week from July 24, they had fields planted with potatoes, corn, beans, peas, and wheat. Most of the people here in the valley were men, and their families were back in Winter Quarters or in other places; so they stayed only a short while, did the planting, and then set out to make the long journey—amounting to distances of 1,000 to 1,300 miles—back to find their families so that at the right time they could all be together in the new gathering place. Brigham Young spent only eighteen days in the Salt Lake Valley and then got on his horse to return to Winter Quarters to get the rest of his family.

By the end of 1847, five months after that first arrival, 423 houses had been built, and the population of the Salt Lake Valley had grown to 1,671.

The first trek of 1847, organized and led by Brigham Young, is described by historians as one of the great epics of United States history. Mormon pioneers by the hundreds suffered and died from disease, exposure, or starvation. There were some who, lacking wagons and teams, literally walked the 1,300 miles across the plains and through the mountains, pushing and pulling hand-carts. In these groups, one in six perished.

During a general conference address on pioneers past and present, Elder Dallin H. Oaks said:

> In a message about the pioneers who crossed the plains over a century ago, President J. Reuben Clark spoke words that apply to pioneers in every age. In his description of "Them of the Last Wagon," President Clark paid tribute to the rank and file, "those great souls, . . . in name unknown, unremembered, unhonored in the pages of history, but lovingly revered round the hearthstones of their children and their children's children" (*J. Reuben Clark: Selected Papers on Religion, Education, and Youth,* ed. David H. Yarn, Jr. [Provo, Utah: Brigham Young Univ. Press, 1984], pp. 67–68; see also *Improvement Era,* Nov. 1947, pp. 704–5, 747–48).
>
> In every great cause there are leaders and followers. In the wagon trains, the leaders were "out in front where the air was clear and clean and where they had unbroken vision of the blue vault of heaven" (*J. Reuben Clark: Selected Papers,* p. 69). But, as President Clark observed, "Back in the last wagon, not always could they see the brethren way out in front and the blue heaven was often shut out from their sight by heavy, dense clouds of the dust of the earth. Yet day after day, they of the last wagon pressed forward, worn and tired, footsore, sometimes almost disheartened, borne up by their faith that God loved them, that the Restored Gospel was true, and that the Lord led and directed the brethren out in front." (Ibid.)

The purposes of God were accomplished by the unswerving loyalty and backbreaking work of the faithful tens of thousands who pushed on, as President Clark said, "with little praise, with not too much encouragement, and never with adulation" (ibid., pp. 69–70).

"And thousands upon thousands of these . . . measured to their humble calling and to their destiny as fully as Brother Brigham and the others measured to theirs, and God will so reward them. They were pioneers in word and thought and act and faith, even as were they of more exalted station. . . . God keep their memories ever fresh among us . . . to help us meet our duties even as they met theirs." (Ibid., pp. 73–74.)

Pointing out that President Clark's words could apply to modern members of the Church as well, Elder Oaks then noted:

In every nation, in every worthy occupation and activity, members of this church face hardships, overcome obstacles, and follow the servants of the Lord Jesus Christ as valiantly as the pioneers of any age. They pay their tithes and offerings. They serve as missionaries or as Church Service volunteers, or they support others who do so. Like the noble young mothers who postpone the pursuit of their personal goals in order to provide the needs of their children, they sacrifice immediate pleasures to keep commitments that are eternal. They accept callings and, in the service of others, they willingly give their time and sometimes their lives.

They do as the Savior taught: They deny themselves; they take up their crosses daily; they follow

Him (see Luke 9:23). These are those the Savior likened to the seed that fell on good ground: "in an honest and good heart, having heard the word, [they] keep it, and bring forth fruit with patience" (Luke 8:15).

The fruits of the gospel issue from every honest and good heart, without regard to past origins or current positions in the Church. As President Clark declared, "There is no aristocracy of birth in this Church; it belongs equally to the highest and the lowliest" (*J. Reuben Clark: Selected Papers*, p. 73). (Dallin H. Oaks, "Modern Pioneers," *Ensign*, November 1989, p. 64.)

Let me relate a little about the lives of some of the pioneers who traveled in the 1840s and 1850s to what is now Utah. We do not know all the challenges and struggles they experienced. But we have glimpses of the difficult times they went through, sometimes from journals or Church records, sometimes through stories passed from generation to generation.

Living conditions were hard, as Daniel Lee Walters tells us. He was born in South Wales in 1843, and as a child traveled with his parents from England to New Orleans by boat, then on to St. Louis, Missouri, by steamboat. They eventually traveled to Kansas, and then across the plains. Once in Salt Lake City, he and his mother walked sixty-five miles to Brigham City, their new home.

Then ten years old, Daniel later wrote of that experience: "My first job on arriving home was to drive two yoke of oxen, breaking new land for spring planting. The crops looked well until August when the grasshoppers came and took all of them. The years 1855 and 56 were the hardest in the history of the county. How we lived through it would be hard to tell. Our main food was bran bread. We ate anything we could get. The cattle were so poor and starved they would freeze while standing. . . . Along toward spring, when the hills began to get bare, we would sharpen sticks and go out and dig segoes for breakfast and dinner. Then go to bed hungry." (*Voices from the Past: Diaries, Journals, and Autobiographies*, 1980 BYU Campus Education Week, p. 50.)

We have many records of the great faith and courage of these pioneers who gathered to Zion. A thirteen-year-old girl was one of these. Mary Goble Pay was born in Brighton, Sussex, England, where her parents joined the Church. Just prior to her thirteenth birthday her parents and five brothers and sisters left their home in England to gather with the Saints in what is now Utah. They traveled to the United States by boat. Despite seasickness, a mutiny on board ship, and thick fog for several days, the family landed safely in Boston, then took the train to Iowa City, where they purchased two yoke of oxen, one yoke of cows, a wagon, and a tent. In Iowa, Mary's little sister, who was suffering from measles, got wet in a fierce thunderstorm and died. She was nearly two years old. They had to bury her there.

Wrote Mary:

We traveled on till we got to the Platt River. That was the last walk I ever had with my mother. We caught up with Handcart companies that day. We watched them cross the river. There were great lumps of ice floating down the river. It was bitter cold. The next morning there were fourteen dead in camp through the cold. We went back to camp and went to prayers. We sang the song "Come, Come, Ye Saints, No Toil Nor Labor Fear." I wondered what made my mother cry. That night my mother took sick and the next morning my little sister was born. . . . We named her Edith and she lived six weeks and died for want of nourishment.

Not long after, Mary went to get some fresh water from a spring for her mother, but got lost in the deep snow. Her legs and feet were frozen by the time the rescuers got to her. They rubbed her legs with snow to revive the circulation and put her feet in a bucket of water. "The pain was so terrible," Mary later wrote. "The frost came out of my legs and feet but did not come out of my toes."

The weather continued to be cruel. During the journey Mary's brother James died, and on the day the family finally arrived in Salt Lake City, 11 December 1856, her mother died.

Mary wrote:

Bishop Hardy had us taken to a home in his ward and the brethren and the sisters brought us plenty of food. We had to be careful and not eat too much as it might kill us we were so hungry.

Early next morning Bro. Brigham Young and a doctor came. . . . When Bro. Young came in he shook hands with us all. When he saw our condition—our feet frozen and our mother dead—tears rolled down his cheeks.

The doctor amputated my toes using a saw and a butcher knife. Brigham Young promised me I would not have to have any more of my feet cut off.

But instead of her feet getting better, Mary's feet got worse. Another doctor advised her to have them amputated at the ankle, but she said no and told him what Brigham Young had promised. The doctor told her there was no chance her feet could be saved. But she had faith.

> One day I sat there crying. My feet were hurting me so—when a little old woman knocked at the door. She said she had felt some one needed her there for a number of days. When she saw me crying she came and asked what was the matter. I showed her my feet and told her the promise Bro. Young had given me. She said, "Yes, and with the help of the Lord we will save them yet." She made a poultice and put on my feet and every day after the doctor had gone she would come and change the poultice. At the end of three months my feet were well.
>
> . . . [The doctor] said that it was a miracle. (From "Mary Goble Pay: Death Strikes the Handcart Company," in *A Believing People: Literature of the Latter-day Saints*, ed. Richard H. Cracroft and Neal E. Lambert [Salt Lake City: Bookcraft, 1979], pp. 105–7.)

I should like to take you back for a moment to the winter of 1848–49 in the Salt Lake Valley. It was a cold winter. There was much of hunger and privation, with the people living on sego bulbs and thistle tops. As spring came, with the burden of preparing the fields for planting and with recollections of the scourge of crickets of the year before, and coincident with the announcement of the discovery of gold on the American River in California, a substantial number of the Saints wanted to move to the gold fields. Some said that they thought Brigham Young too smart a man to try to establish a civilized colony in the barren Salt Lake Valley.

Under those circumstances, President Young said:

We have been kicked out of the frying pan into the fire, and out of the fire into the middle of the floor, and here we are and here we will stay. God has shown me that this is the spot to locate his people, and here is where they will prosper; he will temper the elements for the good of his Saints; he will rebuke the frost and the sterility of the soil, and the land shall become fruitful. . . .

. . . We will extend our settlements to the east and west, to the north and to the south, and we will build towns and cities by the hundreds, and thousands of the Saints will gather in from the nations of the earth. This will become the great highway of the nation. Kings and Emperors and the noble and wise of the earth will visit us here, while the wicked and ungodly will envy us our comfortable homes and possessions. (From autobiography of James Brown, quoted in *Brigham Young: The Man and His Work* [Salt Lake City: Deseret Book Co., 1960], pp. 127-28.)

The pioneer spirit did not stop with those courageous pioneers. We continue to have pioneers around us today. They may not suffer the same physical hardships described in the journals of those faithful Saints who traveled by ox team and handcart, but they have their own hardships, often just as challenging and as refining to their souls. Wrote Henry Ward Beecher, "Affliction comes to us all, not to make us sad, but sober; not to make us sorry, but wise. . . . It is a trial that proves one thing weak and another strong."

Many of us today need that pioneer spirit. I think of mothers who head single-parent families, often working outside the home or struggling to get an education so they can support their children financially. They find hope and sustenance as they rely on those same principles that sustained the Mormon pioneers of the 1840s: faith in God, sacrifice, courage, giving their lives for what they believe.

Laura, thirty-four years old, is an example of this courage. It's not the kind of courage that comes from great acts of bravery like saving the life of a drowning child. It's the quiet, day-to-day kind of courage that comes from sacrificing to create a quality life for her children, ages three and six. Laura was widowed over two years ago. A native of Mexico, she had no skills to earn a living in the United States. After her husband's death, his company went out of business and she lost her pension. She's now working part-time, going to college to earn a degree to teach Spanish in high school, juggling day-care schedules for her children, accepting Church assignments, maintaining her home, cooking and cleaning, and taking time for her children. She typically gets four hours of sleep a night. She has courage and determination. When she was stumped by her algebra class and was failing it, she spent long hours with a tutor to bring up her grade. She ended up with the highest grade in the class on her final—and an A for the course. She has the pioneer spirit—and a great faith to sustain her.

That same sustaining faith can help parents who have struggled with a child gone astray, or young people trying to live moral, clean lives in the midst of trying circumstances and heavy peer pressure, or Church and community leaders earnestly seeking guidance in dealing with problems in their areas of responsibility. That faith can strengthen those who are terminally ill, those facing seemingly insurmountable problems at work, the abused spouse or child, the teenager who in the face of mockery chooses to stand for righteousness, the marriage partners struggling to make their marriage work and choosing persistence and kindness rather than divorce. It can sustain all those who are heavy laden and need rest. Let me tell you about others of these modern-day pioneers who have chosen that path of sustenance.

Maria Flores was called to be Relief Society president in the Tacna Branch of the Peru Lima Mission. But she was afraid she couldn't handle the job, and she fasted and prayed for guidance. She had a dream that night that she was carrying a great weight in her hand and was tired. Then the Savior took the weight from her hands, and said, "Come follow me." As she woke, her fear was gone.

Sister Flores is a seamstress. She writes:

> Every time someone pays me for my work, I set aside one-tenth as my tithing. One time there was no money in the house; I didn't even have one cent other than the money I had set aside for tithing. It was Sunday, and time to pay my tithing at Church.
>
> My son, who was very small at the time, said to me, "But Mama, if you pay your tithing today, what are we going to eat tomorrow?" I told him to have confidence in the Lord and He wouldn't let us go without food. So I went to church, paid my tithing, and came home with peace of mind, but still not knowing what we would do for our next meal, for we had absolutely no money. However, very early the next morning, a lady knocked on my door, bringing me material to make her a dress and paying me in advance for the work, and so we had money to live on the next day.

This woman has courage and faith in God while venturing into unknown territory. Maria Flores has the pioneer spirit.

Let me tell you about another modern-day pioneer, an extremely talented young pianist who had received a call to serve a mission. A newspaper columnist knew of this young man's talent and his call, and wrote a story condemning his decision to accept the call. She wrote:

> He is a brilliant musician, recognized by his teachers and the givers of grants and scholarships as perhaps the best student player of his instrument in the country. I believe that two years away from his practice and his studies at this time will be devastating to his development as a musician.
>
> I have tried to get information from several sources, including a Mormon bishop of our acquaintance, as well as the final decision makers in Salt Lake City. My question is simply this: Why is a mission to a foreign country to convince others that his 'Book of Truth' is truer than theirs more important at this time than his education? How was this decision made?

That young man responded to her question from the mission field. He wrote:

> I am that Mormon missionary who has left his music career and all else to serve in a foreign land and preach the gospel of Jesus Christ to a foreign people. Who I am is not important—what I am doing and how I feel about it are.
>
> I have played the music of the masters since I was in grade school, and have often wondered, "What are they trying to tell me? What are they

saying?'' So many times I have heard a composer's work reach and grope for some theme that is so infinite that it cannot be achieved. But they come close, oh so close. What are they trying to express in this searching? Sometimes they tell us: Beethoven wanted to express joy in his Ninth Symphony. Mahler wanted to express the Resurrection in his Second Symphony. Chopin wanted to express sorrow in his prelude. . . . Through the gospel of Jesus Christ I have found the meaning of these elusive themes, something that most composers could never do. . . . That knowledge springs from my fingers as I play, and the music of those men comes alive with new vitality when I play it. So who am I . . . to say no when that same source of inspiration says, ''Go ye into all the world, and preach the gospel to every creature''? This thing that I have found is so wonderful that I would be a selfish hypocrite to keep it to myself. So now I'm sharing it. And I use music to share it, and I use my words to share it, and I use my love to share it. And now I can say that I have seen a man's life change before my very eyes because of the teachings I preach, and I have seen his joy in this, and I tell you now that that joy is greater than any joy I have ever felt through music. (See *Mesa Tribune,* August 1985.)

This young man with the pioneer spirit follows the same tradition of those pioneers who have gone before him— the courage to devote his life to what he believes, to have faith in God, to turn his life over to God for guidance.

Let me tell you one more story of a modern-day pioneer.

Suzanne Shakespeare was nine years old when she learned she had cancer in her leg. She'd fallen while skating, and the bruise never healed. She ended up at the Primary Children's Hospital in Salt Lake City.

She wrote, "I hated the needles, the doctors, the nurses that came with the needles, the pain in my leg, the wanting to go home when I couldn't."

Her parents knew she had little chance of surviving. They prayed for a miracle, and it happened five years later. The cancer was gone.

"Life was wonderful," said Suzanne. "School was a challenge I loved. I joined clubs, took part in the plays, swam, and rode my bicycle. I had my first real job. . . . Then the hurt came again—the very same leg, the very same place. The swelling began."

Another trip to the hospital, and she learned it was another type of cancer. Her leg must be amputated. She wrote, "September 13, 1978, I lost my left leg about 4 inches above the knee and with it many of the dreams only a sixteen-year-old has. I couldn't decide whether to pray for recovery or for complete oblivion. My world had shattered and I wanted to stop right now—stop because my leg was gone. Stop because I was facing chemotherapy again. . . . What was left?"

But her loving parents helped her accept her problems as a challenge and opportunity—and told her she could triumph. She did. She wrote:

Me, Suzanne Shakespeare, who thought my friends wouldn't like me now and that I wouldn't be able to do anything. I learned something those first few days that is more precious than all my material possessions. I wasn't really different at all. I was still the same girl—the one who joined the clubs and had friends and loved to study. The only thing that had really changed was my capacity to understand and appreciate. . . . And guess what. I've had one date and I'm learning to drive and I'm going to try out for the school musical. I'm getting my new leg soon and I know there will be many hard adjustments ahead. I have had chemotherapy and I've been sick, but I'm alive, and the Lord must have something wonderful ahead just for me.

There were more challenges ahead for her. Later she learned that cancer had spread throughout her lungs. Nothing more could be done by medical science to help her. The next two months she led a busy life, going to a forensics meet, getting a part in the high school musical, attending the sweethearts ball, carrying a full load at school. But she began losing her strength. She took no pain pills, because they would interfere with her activities. Coming home early from a trip with her grandmother, she took her first pain pill, and quietly passed away in her sleep that same evening. (See Jeffrey R. Holland, " 'That Our Children May Know . . . ,' " in *Brigham Young University 1981 Fireside and Devotional Speeches* [Provo, Utah: University Publications, 1981], pp. 158–59.)

Yes, we have a heritage of courage and faith and sacrifice. And the tradition continues every day as we face the problems that life sends our way. Our lives were not meant to be without problems. The pioneers who came to the Salt Lake Valley in 1847 and to Ogden the next year were often tried in the refiner's fire. But despite their trials, they left us a legacy of hope and faith and trust in our Creator. Their example serves as a guide to the generations that follow them.

Like Suzanne Shakespeare, they gained understanding. They learned that the Lord is aware of us and our struggles and that he is there to strengthen us in our trials. The Psalmist tells us, "God is our refuge and strength, a very present help in trouble. Therefore will not we fear." (Psalm 46:1, 2.)

God tells us, "Be still, and know that I am God" (Psalm 46:10).

Allow me to conclude this chapter on a personal note. Each of us with Church pioneer ancestors has roots from which he can draw great strength. Family history research has given me a clearer vision of the blessings that are mine as a result of the faith, courage, and struggles of those who made my blessed heritage in the Church possible.

I have located the ship's manifest of the *Good Ship Olympus*, which sailed from Liverpool, England, in March 1851. My grandfather Joseph S. Lindsay is listed as the youngest child (two years old) of his parents, who came with their five children enroute to Zion. His four oldest siblings had died earlier in the British Isles. The late winter North Atlantic storms caused the ship to nearly founder before a special fast and prayer service of the Saints aboard caused the fury to abate.

Shortly after their arrival in St. Louis by way of New Orleans, my great-grandmother Elizabeth Shanks Lindsay gave birth to her tenth child and youngest son. Within days both she and the baby died leaving John Lindsay alone with his five small children in a new and difficult land. After months of grief and preparation he brought his family to the valley of the Great Salt Lake. Within weeks of their arrival, great-grandfather John, who in earlier life had been a minister of a Protestant denomination in England and who was weakened by the pioneer cross-country trek, himself succumbed to death from an epidemic common to this period.

The five children were now orphans and were left to be raised by various loving Church members who took them into their homes and nurtured them. When my grandfather Joseph Lindsay, who had been but a small child at the death of both his pioneer parents, reached maturity, he married my grandmother Emma Bennion, who was born in Taylorsville in 1851. Together they homesteaded 160 acres of ground and struggled to raise eleven children, including my father, in the faith and testimony of their pioneer parents who gave all they had, including their lives, for the gospel. I now live and have raised my children in a comfortable home in a corner of that homestead once covered by sagebrush and unyielding soil.

I will never live long enough or be able to give enough to express my gratitude to them for their vision and faith and sacrifice. The Lord reassures us with these words: "Fear thou not; for I am with thee: be not dismayed; for I am thy God: I will strengthen thee; yea, I will help thee, yea, I will uphold thee with the right hand of my righteousness" (Isaiah 41:10).

May God bless us to keep the memory of the pioneers and their courage and testimony alive and burning in our own hearts and minds, and especially among our children and grandchildren, who will need their ancestors' courage and vision to get them through a vastly different world but one full of challenges for true young pioneer spirits. God bless the memory of our pioneers and may he fill our hearts and minds with the vision, faith, and courage they possessed.

Come unto Christ

One of the last pleas of the Nephite prophet Moroni was for all men to "come unto Christ and be perfected in him" (Moroni 10:32). This process of coming to Christ includes more than studying the teachings of the Church. It should be the center of our entire existence.

President David O. McKay said, "What you sincerely in your heart think of Christ will determine what you are, and will largely determine what your acts will be" (in Conference Report, April 1951, p. 93).

Elder Bruce R. McConkie described what it means to come unto Christ, to truly worship the Lord:

True and perfect worship consists in following in the steps of the Son of God; it consists in keeping the commandments and obeying the will of the Father to that degree that we advance from grace to grace until we are glorified in Christ as he is in his Father. It is far more than prayer and sermon and song. It is living and doing and obeying. It is emulating the life of the great Exemplar. . . .

To worship the Lord is to follow after him, to seek his face, to believe his doctrine, and to think his thoughts.

It is to walk in his paths, to be baptized as Christ was, to preach that gospel of the kingdom which fell from his lips, and to heal the sick and raise the dead as he did.

To worship the Lord is to put first in our lives the things of his kingdom, to live by every word that proceedeth forth from the mouth of God, to center our whole hearts upon Christ and that salvation which comes because of him.

It is to walk in the light as he is in the light, to do the things that he wants done, to do what he would do under similar circumstances, to be as he is.

To worship the Lord is to walk in the Spirit, to rise above carnal things, to bridle our passions, and to overcome the world.

It is to pay our tithes and offerings, to act as wise stewards in caring for those things which have been entrusted to our care, and to use our talents and means for the spreading of truth and the building up of his kingdom.

To worship the Lord is to be married in the temple, to have children, to teach them the gospel, and to bring them up in light and truth.

It is to perfect the family unit, to honor our father and our mother; it is for a man to love his wife with all his heart and to cleave unto her and none else. ("How to Worship," *Ensign,* December 1971, p. 130.)

Those of us who are priesthood bearers in our homes, I believe, will largely determine the degree to which the blessings of the priesthood will bless and strengthen our own families. Elder Spencer W. Kimball compared the relationship of the Savior to his Church with that of a priesthood bearer to his family as follows: "Christ loved the Church and its people so much that he voluntarily endured persecution for them, suffered humiliating indignities for them, stoically withstood pain and physical abuse for them, and finally gave his precious life for them. When the husband is ready to treat his household in that manner, not only the wife, but also all the family will respond to his leadership." ("Home Training—the Cure for Evil," *Improvement Era,* June 1965, p. 514.)

Elder John A. Widtsoe taught:

The place of woman in the Church is to walk beside the man, not in front of him nor behind him.

In the Church there is full equality between man and woman. The gospel, which is the only concern of the Church, was devised by the Lord for men and women alike. . . .

. . . By divine fiat, the Priesthood is conferred on the men. This means that organization must prevail in the family, the ultimate unit of the Church. The husband, the Priesthood bearer, presides over the family; the Priesthood conferred upon him is intended for the blessing of the whole family. Every member shares in the gift bestowed, but under a proper organization. No man who understands the gospel believes that he is greater than his wife, or more beloved of the Lord, because he holds the Priesthood. (*Improvement Era,* March 1942, pp. 161, 188; also in *Evidences and Reconciliations,* arr. G. Homer Durham [Salt Lake City: Bookcraft, 1987] pp. 305, 307–8.)

President David O. McKay, speaking to a group of priesthood brethren on the importance of the work in which they were engaged, counseled them as follows:

Let me assure you, brethren, that some day you will have a personal priesthood interview with the Savior himself. If you are interested, I will tell you the order in which he will ask you to account for your earthly responsibilities.

First, he will request an accountability report about your relationship with your wife. Have you actively been engaged in making her happy and ensuring that her needs have been met as an individual?

Second, he will want an accountability report about each of your children individually. He will not attempt to have this for simply a family stewardship but will request information about your relationship to each and every child.

Third, he will want to know what you personally have done with the talents you were given in the preexistence.

Fourth, he will want a summary of your activity in your Church assignments. He will not be necessarily interested in what assignments you have had, for in his eyes the home teacher and a mission president are probably equals, but he will request a summary of how you have been of service to your fellowman in your Church assignments.

Fifth, he will have no interest in how you earned your living but if you were honest in all your dealings.

Sixth, he will ask for an accountability on what you have done to contribute in a positive manner to your community, state, country, and the world. (As quoted in Stephen R. Covey, *The Divine Center* [Salt Lake City: Bookcraft, 1982], pp. 54–55.)

President Joseph F. Smith counseled the Saints:

Let love, and peace, and the Spirit of the Lord, kindness, charity, sacrifice for others, abound in your families. Banish harsh words, envyings, hatreds, evil speaking, obscene language and innuendo, blasphemy, and let the Spirit of God take possession of your hearts. Teach to your children these things, in spirit and power, sustained and strengthened by personal practice. Let them see that you are earnest, and practice what you preach. (*Gospel Doctrine* [Salt Lake City: Deseret Book Co., 1939], p. 302.)

The family is the strongest unit of society and the unit of highest responsibility. To break down this strength is ultimately to break down civilization itself. If men are not made to feel their obligations to home and family, they cannot be made to feel their obligations to anyone or anything—and soon this selfishness and irresponsibility make their inroads upon communities and nations.

Brethren, we can further bless our families by building each family member. Our wives and children should be made to feel good about themselves. Wives and children so praised and appreciated will be more appreciative and loving in return. In these stressful times we cannot ignore the need to spend sufficient quality time with our families—to really listen and convey the message, "I respect you enough to listen to what you say." Such commitment to promote the happiness of each family member will pay rich rewards in genuine gospel-centered family living.

To paraphrase the prophet Malachi, when the hearts of the fathers are *truly* turned to the children, only then will the hearts of the children turn to their fathers.

To follow the Lord is to visit the fatherless and the widows in their affliction and to keep ourselves un-spotted from the world.

A few years ago a ninety-year-old patriarch, the son of a prophet, was quietly laid to rest in the Salt Lake Valley. For forty-seven years of my own mother's wid-owhood, this gentle soul regularly visited our fatherless family to offer wise counsel and priesthood blessings to our family, first comprised of young children and later of maturing adults. His personal concern, coupled with the goodness of many other worthy priesthood leaders, pro-vided the strength and example to our family to face the problems of the Great Depression, wars, and the many other worldly influences and daily problems with which each of us must cope. This same effort was extended to numerous families within the acquaintanceship of this good and holy man.

I express my heartfelt gratitude for those whose influ-ence reached beyond their own homes and touched and strengthened me. I'm grateful for the opportunity to serve and perhaps to repay in small measure what I owe to so many for wise counsel and influence.

I return now to the words of Elder McConkie on com-ing unto and worshiping the Lord:

> [To worship the Lord] is to work on a welfare project, to administer to the sick, to go on a mis-

sion, to go home teaching, and to hold family home evening.

To worship the Lord is to study the gospel, to treasure up light and truth, to ponder in our hearts the things of his kingdom, and to make them part of our lives.

It is to pray with all the energy of our souls, to preach by the power of the Spirit, to sing songs of praise and thanksgiving.

To worship is to work, to be actively engaged in a good cause, to be about our Father's business, to love and serve our fellowmen.

It is to feed the hungry, to clothe the naked, to comfort those that mourn, and to hold up the hands that hang down and to strengthen the feeble knees.

To worship the Lord is to stand valiantly in the cause of truth and righteousness, to let our influence for good be felt in civic, cultural, educational, and governmental fields, and to support those laws and principles which further the Lord's purposes on earth.

To worship the Lord is to be of good cheer, to be courageous, to be valiant, to have the courage of our God-given convictions, and to keep the faith. ("How to Worship," p. 130.)

President Hugh B. Brown related this inspiring story: Some time ago a great actor in the city of New York gave a wonderful performance in a large theatre, at the close of which there were rounds of applause. He was called back again and again. Finally someone called to him, "Would you do for us the twenty-third Psalm?"

"Why, yes, I know the twenty-third Psalm."

He recited it as an actor would, perfectly, with nothing left to be desired as far as a performance was concerned. When he was finished, again there was thunderous applause. Then the actor came to the front of the stage and said: "Ladies and gentlemen, there is an old man sitting here on the front row whom I happen to know. I am going to ask him without any notice if he will come and repeat the twenty-third Psalm."

The elderly gentleman, of course, was frightened. Trembling, he came to the stage. Fearfully he looked out over the vast audience. Then, as though he were at home with only one, he closed his eyes against the audience, bowed his head, and talked to God, and said:

The Lord is my shepherd; I shall not want.

He maketh me to lie down in green pastures: he leadeth me beside the still waters.

He restoreth my soul: he leadeth me in the paths of righteousness for his name's sake.

Then, changing to address the Savior directly and intimately, he continued:

Yea, though I walk through the valley of the shadow of death, I will fear no evil: for thou art with me; thy rod and thy staff they comfort me.

Thou preparest a table before me in the presence of mine enemies: thou anointest my head with oil; my cup runneth over.

Surely goodness and mercy shall follow me all the days of my life: and I will dwell in the house of the Lord forever.

When the old man finished, there was no applause, but there was not a dry eye in that house. The actor came to the front of the stage. He too was wiping his eyes. And he said, "Ladies and gentlemen, I know the *words* of the twenty-third Psalm, but this man knows the Shepherd." (Adapted from Hugh B. Brown, *Continuing the Quest* [Salt Lake City: Deseret Book Co., 1961], pp. 335–36.)

May we truly come to know Jesus Christ, whose example we seek to follow.

Two Kinds
of Learning

Learning is an eternal value. I know of nothing more central to eternal progress. We know that whatever degree of intelligence we attain in this life, "it will rise with us in the resurrection" (D&C 130:18). Note that the word is *intelligence,* which I submit is broader in its meaning than either *information* or *knowledge.* In the eternal scheme of things it may or may not be important for you to know the elements of tort law, or the second law of thermodynamics. But what is important is that you be able to use the learning tools by which you come to an understanding of tort law, the second law of thermodynamics, and so on.

What, then, are the tools we use to comply with the biblical injunction to gain understanding, and what are the processes that will make us happier people in this life?

In my view, those processes can be divided into two categories. We might refer to them as the rational process and the extra-rational process. The rational process is the one used the most in school studies. Its components are familiar to all: reading, analysis, written and oral expression, research, criticism, and skepticism.

In several ways, the extra-rational process is different. Its methods are not the same. The results, however, when properly employed and properly interpreted, are much more sure. The process is not available to everyone. Neither is it as susceptible to individual human control. It is, however, a superior process.

For centuries prior to 1820, human beings had debated the nature of God. On occasion, hundreds of the world's best scholars had assembled for the purpose of resolving the issue by application of their combined intellectual talents. Out of centuries of rational effort, then, evolved the prevailing Christian concept of Deity. And yet in the space of just a few minutes, a boy of fourteen years learned more about the true nature of God than had come from centuries of the best rational effort of the world's finest minds. It did not result from debate, analysis, criticism, or human intellectual exchange. The process was extra-rational. It came through revelation.

I would like to explore some of the relationships between these two great learning processes and the significance of those relationships to our happiness and progress in this life and the next.

These two processes, properly understood, are not mutual antagonists. On the contrary, I believe that both the scriptures and human experience identify them as complementary and mutually supportive.

However, it should come as no surprise to anyone that some people develop more proficiency with one of these processes than with the other. It is a predictable but nonetheless unfortunate consequence that those who feel more comfortable with one of them are frequently inclined to downplay or even be suspicious of the other. Worst of all, they may tend to ridicule or even stop using the method with which they feel less comfortable or are less proficient. Thus, we find some people completely rejecting understanding that is not rational in origin or rationally verifiable. Equally regrettable, on the other end of the spectrum, is the view that higher education and the tools that it employs are to be distrusted and avoided.

Those attitudes are not only wrong but also reflective of a fundamental misunderstanding of the scriptures and of the foundational eternal objective to pursue the acquisition of knowledge and understanding. Section 88 of the Doctrine and Covenants is explicit on this point. It does not enjoin us to seek "either by study or by faith." Neither does it admonish that "if ye have achieved learning by faith, ye are thereby permanently exempt from study." Rather, the commandment is to obtain learning and to obtain it "by study and also by faith" (D&C 88:118). The plain message is that the two are companions, not antagonists—that no person is truly learned whose learning experiences exclude either the rational or the extra-rational method.

The famous instruction given to Oliver Cowdery in section 9 of the Doctrine and Covenants also involves a combination of the two processes: "You must study it out in your mind; then you must ask me if it be right, and if it is right I will cause that your bosom shall burn within you; therefore, you shall feel that it is right" (D&C 9:8).

There are differences in the two processes. For one, the driving force is the spirit, and for the other, the mind. One is more reliable—that is, if it leads to divine sources—and the other is more deliberate and more subject to human control.

But both are means to the same end. The true intellectual is one whose intellect is sufficiently developed that he recognizes not only the great potential but also the limitations of his intellectual capacity. There is no need for the person who has acquired understanding through spiritual insights to be suspicious of those who acquire learning by study. The most learned people I know are people who find no inconsistency between study and faith and who have achieved proficiency in each. We should feel equally at home in the academy and in the temple. We should regard each as a center of learning. We know that the day will come when the lamb will lie down with the lion. We need not await the Millennium for the scholar to be a patriarch, and the patriarch a scholar.

One of the surest marks of the intellectually mature person is a willingness to try to understand a point of view with which he or she disagrees. John Stuart Mill said that he who knows only his own case knows little of that.

The truly learned person—of any profession—is one who is willing to try to understand to the best of his ability the opposing viewpoint, not just in the sense of being able to state what it is but also in the sense of genuinely attempting to comprehend its merit. That kind of attitude about a position with which you disagree is, I believe, nothing more than a manifestation of the admonition stated in so many of the Savior's teachings that we should be concerned about others and not just ourselves.

The true Samaritan, the person who is genuinely concerned about his neighbor, is sensitive not just to his neighbor's physical needs—food, clothing, and shelter—but to his thoughts as well.

The final relationship that I will discuss between these two great learning processes is perhaps the most important: What should a person do when these two processes yield different results? It doesn't happen very often, and in fact for some it may never occur. But for others, during the course of their lives there may occur instances in which their mental processes lead to a conclusion that they know is wrong because it is at odds with revealed truth. On those rare occasions when this happens, what should a person do?

First, let me say what he should *not* do. He should not reject the value of intellectual effort—dismissing it as the process that brought him to a conclusion that by definition has to be wrong.

It would be an erroneous and unfortunate oversimplification to say that intellectual effort—including such necessary components as skepticism and objectivity—is to be avoided because it can and sometimes does lead to conclusions that are at odds with eternal values. The reason that this would be both unfortunate and erroneous is that intellectual effort—including that which occasionally leads to error—is itself an eternal value. In the dispute that preceded the War in Heaven, one thing that everyone appeared to recognize was that under the Lord's plan, some mistakes would be made. Indeed, the discretion to make choices, some of which by definition would be wrong, is the distinctive characteristic of the plan we chose.

One older Church member once said to a younger man who had lost his testimony while attending college: "If I had a boy like you, I'd send him through the world in illiteracy rather than see him lose his eternal soul."

If that were the choice, what a tragedy it would be! But as I understand the gospel, that is not the choice. The choice is not between literacy and the eternal soul. The latter cannot exist without the former. It would therefore be the gravest error, in the name of things eternal, to say that careful, objective, critical, even skeptical intellectual effort is to be avoided because on occasion it can lead to disastrous results. That kind of rational effort is itself divinely ordained as the cornerstone of the plan we all chose when we kept our first estate. What should we do, then, when our rational processes lead to a conclusion inconsistent with revealed truth?

The answer to that question can be fairly simply stated. Since the rational process is subject to human error and revealed truth is not, over the interim period (which could extend beyond the term of this life), until we can confirm through our own intellectual faculties that which has come through a more sure source, we simply recognize that it *is* a more sure source and that our inability to reach a reconciliation is only another indication of the imperfection of the human intellect.

I want to caution that that principle is necessarily premised on the existence of a genuine conflict between the products of, on the one hand, rational processes and, on the other, extra-rational processes that amount to revealed truth. My experience as a stake president taught me to be cautious in that respect. It is not uncommon for individuals to obtain what they perceive to be divine confirmation, when in fact the process, while truly extra-rational, involves only an emotional support for an answer that was based on nothing but emotion in the first place.

Let me give an example. I don't smoke tobacco, and I don't drink alcohol. The question of whether I would smoke or drink, even in moderation or on isolated occasions, for the achievement of social or business objectives, or even when no one was watching, is simply not an open question. The answer to that question was definitively provided for me by God himself in a revelation given to Joseph Smith on 27 February 1833. Even if I should conclude, through the utilization of my reasoning powers, that I would be a happier person if I smoked, and that the delightful smell on my clothes—and the aura of distinction and dignity that surrounds smokers—is more important than ten or fifteen years added on to my life, I still would not smoke. Similarly, I don't need to concern myself with whether eight years of age is the best age for baptism or whether there really ought to be seventeen Apostles.

For people who are convinced of the reality of the Restoration, conflicts between revealed truth and reasoned conclusions are so rare as to be virtually nonexistent. But I am also telling you that it is no adverse reflection on you, on your mind or on your soul or on your values, if on some occasion you are unable to explain rationally a principle of revealed truth. The seeming inconsistency is attributable only to the fallible nature of our rational capacity. It tells us nothing more than that there are some facts, some truths, some realities which our mortal minds at this time are simply unable to comprehend.

Fortunately, the fact that some truths are beyond mortal comprehension is something that our minds can comprehend. As a simple example, let us consider the proposition that space is without end. My brain is unable to comprehend that fact. I simply lack the capacity to perceive how it is that space can continue on and on and never come to an end. And yet my mind is sufficiently developed to comprehend that the alternative is totally unacceptable. If there is some point out there where it all comes to an end, then the question is,

What's on the other side? These questions concerning space, and their equally perplexing counterparts relating to time (and the concept of time's having no beginning or end), supply examples demonstrating the limitations of the rational process.

Our minds are good enough to recognize their own shortcomings. That ought to alert us that in those instances where our minds lead us to a conclusion inconsistent with truth that comes from a source not subject to those same shortcomings, there is no doubt which should prevail.

Learning, then, whether by rational or by extrarational processes, is an essential part of our development as children of God. As such it can not only prove to be of inestimable worth to our eternal souls but also bring delight and joy to our daily lives.

CHAPTER SEVENTEEN

The Spirit
Matters Most

In this chapter I should like to discuss walking in the Spirit. Paul, in writing to the Romans, counseled "that the righteousness of the law might be fulfilled in us, who walk not after the flesh, but after the Spirit" (Romans 8:4).

Moroni says that all spiritual gifts "come by the Spirit of Christ" (Moroni 10:17). The Spirit of Christ "giveth light to every man that cometh into the world" (D&C 84:46). It "is given to every man, that he may know good from evil" (Moroni 7:16). By this means every son and daughter of God has "the light" to judge what is right and to seek to "lay hold upon every good thing" (Moroni 7:18–19). By this Spirit, all may seek to learn of God and to exercise faith in him. Enlightened by this Spirit, all may seek spiritual gifts, which, as

Moroni says, "come unto every man severally, according as he will" (Moroni 10:17).

Faith is a spiritual gift. So is personal revelation. So is a testimony of Jesus Christ. And there are other spiritual gifts. We know too little about spiritual gifts.

As men and women desire to believe, they develop faith in God (see Alma 32:26–43). When they have enough faith, they can receive a manifestation of the Holy Ghost. The Book of Mormon has such an account in Alma 18–19.

Ammon preached to the Lamanite king Lamoni. When the king believed and cried to the Lord for mercy, he fell to the earth as if he were dead. After two days Lamoni's people were about to bury him, but the queen, hearing that Ammon was a prophet, called for him and asked him to go in to see the King again. This he did, and then told the queen that Lamoni would revive on the morrow. The queen believed him, and Ammon called her blessed because of her "exceeding faith" (Alma 19:10).

When King Lamoni arose, he blessed the name of God and prophesied that the Redeemer would be born of a woman and would "redeem all mankind who believe[d] on his name." Afterwards, he and the queen and Ammon sank down, overpowered by the Spirit. After the people had assembled, the queen arose first. She "cried with a loud voice, saying: O blessed Jesus, who has saved me from an awful hell! O blessed God, have mercy on this people!" Ammon baptized King Lamoni, the queen, and many of their people. (Alma 19:12–35.)

Elder Bruce R. McConkie declared at the dedication of the Nauvoo Monument to Women:

> Where spiritual things are concerned, as pertaining to all of the gifts of the Spirit, with refer-

ence to the receipt of revelation, the gaining of testimonies, and the seeing of visions, in all matters that pertain to godliness and holiness and which are brought to pass as a result of personal righteousness—in all these things men and women stand in a position of absolute equality before the Lord. He is no respecter of persons nor of sexes, and he blesses those men and those women who seek him and serve him and keep his commandments. ("Our Sisters from the Beginning," *Ensign*, January 1979, p. 61.)

Spiritual gifts do not always come automatically and immediately with the gift of the Holy Ghost. The Prophet Joseph Smith taught that many such gifts are "not visible to the natural vision, or understanding of man," and that it "require[s] time and circumstances to call these gifts into operation" (*Teachings of the Prophet Joseph Smith*, comp. Joseph Fielding Smith [Salt Lake City: Deseret Book Co., 1976], pp. 244, 246).

The scriptures tell us that we should desire and zealously seek spiritual gifts (see D&C 46:8; 1 Corinthians 12:31; 14:1, 11). We are also told that some will receive one gift and some will receive another (see D&C 46:11; 1 Corinthians 12; Moroni 10:8–18). In every case, the receipt of spiritual gifts is predicated upon faith, obedience, and personal righteousness.

Spiritual gifts are evidently among the "signs [that] shall follow them that believe" (Mark 16:17).

We are commanded not to seek for signs to develop our faith (see Matthew 12:39; D&C 63:12), for "faith cometh not by signs" (D&C 63:9). But when we have faith, repent, and are born of water and the Spirit, and when we love and serve God with all our hearts, we are eligible to receive spiritual gifts. We may then, as Paul taught, "covet earnestly the best gifts" (1 Corinthians 12:31; see also D&C 46:8).

When we believe and seek spiritual gifts to benefit others "and not for a sign" (D&C 46:9), we are told that signs will follow. "Behold, . . . signs follow those that believe. Yea, signs come by faith, not by the will of men, nor as they please, but by the will of God. Yea, signs come by faith, unto mighty works." (D&C 63:9–11).

Let us consider some of these spiritual gifts.

Faith is a gift of the Spirit. As Alma taught, the gift takes root in our hearts as hope and, nurtured as a seedling, will eventually flower as knowledge and bear the fruit of eternal life (see Alma 32:26–43).

Elder A. Theodore Tuttle, in his last conference address delivered shortly before his death in 1986, gave us the following wonderful testimony of his own faith. At the time he gave this talk he was dying of cancer.

I recall that when I was twenty years old, I went for an interview with the bishop to go on a mission. When I returned, my mother, all smiles, said, "Well, Ted, what did the bishop say?"

"He said I couldn't go."

"Why not?" my mother asked.

And I said, "Because we don't have enough money."

[She said,] "If my father could leave two children and another to be born shortly after he left, you can go."

I said, "I know that, but the bishop doesn't."

Parenthetically, I might say that he was doing his job right. He asked me if I had any money. I told him I had a few hundred dollars that I had earned that summer.

He said, "Then what?"

I said, "My dad will send it to me."

He said, "Does your dad have it?"

I said, "No," and he didn't. We had lost our sheep herd during the Depression. My father was a livestock dealer buying lambs and wool on commission, and that was a very uncertain income.

The bishop said, "The Brethren have had some serious experiences, and so you cannot go unless you can guarantee that you'll have sufficient money."

I accepted that, and that's what I told my mother.

That night we waited for Dad to come home and then held a family council. We concluded that we didn't then have enough money—and that we wouldn't, so far as we could see, anytime in the future. We decided to ask our neighbor, Tom Anderson, a rather wealthy man, if he would help. When we explained our situation, he said, "You tell the bishop that I will 'back you.' "

Before the bishop opened his business the next morning, I was there waiting to tell him that Tom Anderson said he would back me. The bishop said, "That's all I need to know."

The interesting thing was that we never did have to call on Brother Anderson. My folks would send that check and with it a note, "This is for this month, and we'll have the next month's, too."

I am a product of a household of faith. I learned faith in my home. I was taught it. It was drilled into me. I need that faith now as much as I ever did.

I think we all do. We're not going to survive in this world, temporally or spiritually, without increased faith in the Lord—and I don't mean a positive mental attitude—I mean downright solid faith in the Lord Jesus Christ. That is the one thing that gives vitality and power to otherwise rather weak individuals.

I bear you my humble witness that I know that God lives. I know that he lives, that he is our Father, that he loves us. I bear witness that Jesus is the Christ, our Savior and our Redeemer.

I understand better what that means now. I am grateful for his atonement in our behalf and for knowing something about our relationship to him and to our Heavenly Father and about the meaning and purpose of the gospel of Jesus Christ. I am grateful for Joseph Smith. I know he was a prophet, and I know that President Ezra Taft Benson is a living prophet today. I bear that witness in the name of Jesus Christ, amen. ("Developing Faith," *Ensign,* November 1986, p. 73.)

Another familiar spiritual gift is the gift of testimony. "To some it is given by the Holy Ghost to know that Jesus Christ is the Son of God, and that he was crucified for the sins of the world" (D&C 46:13). Many Latter-day Saints have this gift.

Others have a related gift, as shown by these two verses in section 46 of the Doctrine and Covenants: "To some it is given by the Holy Ghost to know that Jesus Christ is the Son of God. . . . To others it is given to believe on their words, that they also might have eternal life if they continue faithful." (D&C 46:13–14.)

Since it is given to some to know and to others to believe on their words, those who know must be responsible for sharing their testimonies. Only in this way can they give those who have the gift of believing on their words something to lean upon as they too move toward eternal life.

The relationship between these gifts illustrates the purpose for which all spiritual gifts are given. "And all these gifts come from God, for the benefit of the children of God" (D&C 46:26). Spiritual gifts are given to members of the Church "that all may be profited thereby" (D&C 46:12; see also D&C 46:9; Moroni 10:8). The same principle is evident in Paul's teachings in 1 Corinthians 12. Here spiritual gifts are likened to the various parts of the body, each performing its own function and each serving the entire "body of Christ" (1 Corinthians 12:27).

Another spiritual gift mentioned in the Bible, the Book of Mormon, and the Doctrine and Covenants is the gift of being able to "teach the word of knowledge by the same Spirit" (Moroni 10:10; see also Alma 9:21; D&C 46:18). Many have received this gift, and we have all been blessed by its exercise.

The spiritual gift referred to as the "word of wisdom" (see D&C 46:17; Moroni 10:9; 1 Corinthians 12:8) has been explained as the wise application of knowledge. We might call this judgment. This is a precious gift for any field of knowledge, but judgment in applying spiritual knowledge is a quality of eternal worth.

To others is given the gift of "faith to be healed" (D&C 46:19). Most of us know people who have been healed miraculously. Many of these healings are attributable, at least in part, to the afflicted person's gift of faith to be healed.

Another spiritual gift is "faith to heal" (D&C 46:20; see also Moroni 10:11; 1 Corinthians 12:9; *Teachings of the Prophet Joseph Smith*, pp. 224–25). This gift has an obvious relationship to priesthood administration to the sick.

A more familiar gift of the Spirit is personal revelation. Alma described the universal character of this spiritual gift. "And now, he imparteth his word by angels unto men, yea, not only men but women also. Now this is not all; little children do have words given unto them many times, which confound the wise and the learned." (Alma 32:23).

There is a choice example of personal revelation in the twenty-fifth chapter of Genesis. When Rebekah was carrying the twins Jacob and Esau, "the children struggled together within her." The scripture says she was troubled at this and so "she went to enquire of the Lord." (Genesis 25:22.)

Here we see a major principle of revelation. It usually comes in response to earnest prayer. "Ask, and it shall be given you; seek, and ye shall find; knock, and it shall be opened unto you" (Matthew 7:7).

In this instance the Lord spoke to Rebekah, saying: "Two nations are in thy womb, and two manner of people shall be separated from thy bowels; and the one people shall be stronger than the other people; and the elder shall serve the younger" (Genesis 25:23). Though she was the wife of a prophet and patriarch, Rebekah inquired of the Lord and the Lord instructed her directly on a matter of great personal concern to her, to the children she would bear, and to generations unborn. After recounting this incident, Elder Bruce R. McConkie concluded, "The Lord gives revelation to women who pray to him in faith" ("Mothers in Israel and Daughters of Zion," *New Era*, May 1978, p. 36).

We should seek after spiritual gifts. They can lead us to God. They can shield us from the power of the adversary. They can compensate for our inadequacies and repair our imperfections. Almost a century ago President George Q. Cannon of the First Presidency taught the Saints:

If any of us are imperfect, it is our duty to pray for the gift that will make us perfect. . . . No man ought to say, "Oh, I cannot help this; it is my nature." He is not justified in it, for the reason that God has promised to give strength to correct these things, and to give gifts that will eradicate them. If a man lack wisdom, it is his duty to ask God for wisdom. The same with everything else. That is the design of God concerning His Church. He wants His Saints to be perfected in the truth. For this purpose He gives these gifts, and bestows them upon those who seek after them, in order that they may be perfect people upon the face of the earth. (*Deseret Evening News,* 23 December 1893, pt. 2, p. 9.)

I saw that principle in action in the home in which I was raised. Having lost her husband, my mother was incomplete. How she prayed for what she needed to fulfill her responsibility to raise her small children! She was seeking, she was worthy, and she was surely blessed! Her prayers were answered in many ways, and I believe she received special spiritual gifts. The ones that stand out in my memory are the gifts of faith, testimony, and wisdom. She was a devoted daughter in Zion, and her life exemplified—in its own way—the fulfillment of Lehi's promise to his son Jacob that God "shall consecrate thine afflictions for thy gain" (2 Nephi 2:2).

Examples of walking by the Spirit are all around us. May God bless you that you may walk in the Spirit of the Savior and thereby bless your own lives and your own families and all the families with whom you come in contact.

Easy Yoke and
Light Burden

During his mortal ministry, the Savior
sometimes made what we would consider to be paradox-
ical statements. One such statement is his invitation:
"Take my yoke upon you. . . . For my yoke is easy and
my burden is light." (Matthew 11:29–30.) The words
yoke and *burden* suggest heaviness, oppression, something difficult to bear. How can yokes be easy, burdens
light?

If I were to ask you a question from one of our
popular hymns—"Are you ever burdened?" ("Count
Your Blessings," *Hymns*, no. 241)—the answer would
likely be a resounding yes from most of you. None of us
has escaped or will escape life's heavy burdens. One of
Job's counselors reminded him that "man is born unto
trouble, as the sparks fly upward" (Job 5:7). The com-

mon lot of being born into mortality is to be burdened "with a load of care" (*Hymns*, no. 241). Each of us will have a share of life's pain, disappointment, sickness, sorrow, loneliness, frustration, aging, and finally the specter of death. I have a four-year-old grandson who says repeatedly but good naturedly, with a smile on his face, "Grandpa, life is tough, and then you die."

Added to the common lot of burdens, we who have been yoked to the gospel way of life have additional burdens. We carry the economic burden of tithing, fast offerings, missionary funds. We carry the physical burdens that a lay church imposes. There is no paid ministry to do our home teaching, our visiting teaching, our welfare assignments, our compassionate service. Other gospel-related burdens may include writing in journals, attending temple sessions, and doing genealogical research, as well as our fulfilling particular Church callings. Beyond these specific laws and commandments, the Doctrine and Covenants reminds us that we "should be anxiously engaged in a good cause, and do many things of [our] own free will, and bring to pass much righteousness" (D&C 58:27).

We also bear the psychological burden of being a peculiar people. Some of us have faced ridicule and persecution for our beliefs. Some of us have likely borne the emotional burden of estrangement from lifelong friends and from family members who do not share our faith. Others have borne the sorrow of seeing family members choose a different way of life than our church has taught. There is, too, the great burden of disappointment we feel when we see that some fellow Saints lie, cheat, steal, gossip, and are short-tempered, unloving, and impatient. There is the greater burden of disappointment if we find that we ourselves can also lie, cheat, steal, gossip, or are short-tempered, unloving, and impatient. There is the additional burden of disappointment when we realize that a community of Saints is not always as readily distinguishable from other communities of faith.

These are some of the gospel burdens we all carry. What of the greater burden of our Church leaders, who carry additional responsibilities? Perhaps they feel at times like Moses, who was asked to lead the Israelites. He expressed his feelings about the heaviness of the burden of leadership when he answered the Lord: "Wherefore hast thou afflicted thy servant . . . that thou layest the burden of all this people upon me? Have I conceived all this people? have I begotten them? . . . I am not able to bear all this people alone, because it is too heavy for me." (Numbers 11:11-12, 14.)

I find nowhere in the scriptures a promise that we will be without burdens, that the yoke of the gospel is to be taken from us. But there is the Savior's promise that his yoke can be easy, his burden light. How can this be?

May I suggest four ways that may help to lighten our burden:

1. First, if we adequately value the burden we are carrying, if we know it is the pearl of great price that will enrich each step of the way, much of its heaviness will seem to disappear. I submit that the burden of a meaningless existence, or a life without purpose, is heavier than all that the gospel requires and inspires us to carry. If faith is a burden—and it is—doubt or disbelief is the greater burden.

2. The Lord tells us of another sure way to lighten our burden and to ease the yoke. He says: "Bear ye one another's burdens, and so fulfill the law of Christ" (Galatians 6:2). Here is another paradox. If we add others' burdens to ours, doesn't it seem reasonable that we shall have a heavier load? Not so. Being aware of

others' burdens and helping carry them lightens both their burdens and our own. The classic reply captured in a popular song, "He's not heavy—he's my brother," explains this otherwise illogical conclusion. The wonderful plan that provides that we are born into loving families lightens burdens. As family members our love grows as we carry our burdens together. And so it can be in the larger family of ward and stake if we will bear one another's burdens.

3. A third way to lighten our burden is to throw off yesterday's load and not prematurely take up tomorrow's load. A kind plan hides the future and its heavy burdens from us all and allows us, through the principle of repentance, to leave yesterday's burdens behind, learning its lessons but not being borne down by useless regrets. We need to remember that "yard by yard, life's hard; inch by inch, life's a cinch."

4. Finally, to ease the burdens which all of us bear, we are counseled in Psalm 55:22, "Cast thy burden upon the Lord, and he shall sustain thee: he shall never suffer the righteous to be moved." Many of us have experienced this sustaining power.

Indeed, most Latter-day Saints reach a point at some time or times when they realize that there is no other place to turn to, no other being upon whom to "cast our burdens," except the Savior.

Thus the one sure solution to the myriad problems of these difficult times is actually simple, yet deeply profound: we must turn to the Savior. He is always there. His comfort and his wisdom are offered freely. He will sustain us.

"Ye Have Done It unto Me"

As I have met with various Church members in my capacity as a General Authority, I have gained a broader vision of the Savior's words as recorded in Matthew:

> Then shall the righteous answer him, saying, Lord, when saw we thee an hungred, and fed thee? or thirsty, and gave thee drink?
>
> When saw we thee a stranger, and took thee in? or naked, and clothed thee?
>
> Or when saw we thee sick, or in prison, and came unto thee?
>
> And the King shall answer and say unto them, Verily I say unto you, Inasmuch as ye have done it unto one of the least of these my brethren, ye have done it unto me. (Matthew 25:37–40.)

In visits to several stakes of Zion, my life has been blessed and my faith has been increased as I have observed and experienced the Christlike love and the quiet, unheralded service demonstrated in the lives of countless true Latter-day Saints.

Such examples of charity, the pure love of Christ, are not restricted to geographic location, age, gender, or station in life. Such acts of kindness and love of fellowman seek no praise or reward and are often performed within the humble homes and from the loving hearts of the Lord's devoted servants.

Permit me to recount a few such examples from the lives of true followers of Christ.

In connection with a stake conference assignment, Elder James M. Paramore and I were blessed to visit the home of a dear brother who, in a tragic industrial accident on August 26, 1958, fell from a cooling tower into a hole thirty-five feet below, where he landed on his head and became paralyzed from the shoulders down. In the intervening years he has survived as one of the longest-living quadriplegics in medical history. He was unable to attend the conference meetings, but a brief, thoughtfully prepared video of his life and testimony was presented in the Saturday evening session of conference. He lies not in a bed but suspended on a circular metal rack, where he has received devoted nursing care twenty-four hours a day, seven days a week, since this accident in 1958.

This brother, whose home we visited following the conference, praised his nurses, his priesthood leaders, his home teachers, and many others who during those long years stood by his side and ministered to his spiritual and temporal needs. A wise stake president had called him to be the regular correspondent to the missionaries and the servicemen from his stake. I have been inspired many times as I have read his letters sent to bolster the faith of choice young missionaries across the world.

May I quote two lines from one of these missionary letters: "Christ is the only way to heaven. All other paths are detours to doom—commitment to Christ should go hand in hand with commitment to his Church."

In another stake, in a Sunday morning Primary meeting of stake conference, I met two beautiful daughters of a faithful young Latter-day Saint physician and his devoted wife. The older child was in a wheelchair, and her younger sister moved with great effort. Both children suffer from a degenerative disease of genetic origin thought to be progressive and incurable. According to medical wisdom, their time in this life is extremely limited. Their eyes were beautiful and clear—full of faith and love of their Savior, whose presence had been made real in their lives by loving parents, grandparents, and teachers.

To fulfill a deep desire for more children, their devoted parents have adopted two other beautiful daughters from another country. Instead of cursing God as Job was encouraged by his associates to do in the face of similar faith-testing burdens, this couple has reached out to these two beautiful additional daughters, who now feel the blessing of being reared in a household of faith, with love from parents whose hearts and lives demonstrate the pure love of Christ.

Following a stake conference in another area, Sister Lindsay and I were blessed to visit another household of faith located in rural Idaho. The young father in this home was suffering from a critical illness. A picture forever etched in my memory is of a mother and five beautiful young children, together with this dear brother's priesthood quorum leaders, kneeling around his bedside pleading with Heavenly Father for the life of this good man. He was then administered to within this circle of faith. Later it was our blessing again to meet this young couple and to hear their beautiful witnessing, their humbling outpouring of spirit, of the Lord's blessings in the restoration of the husband's health.

In yet another stake conference, a dear sister confined to a wheelchair testified to the strength she received from feeling the Lord's love through reading the Book of Mormon. Earlier her devoted husband had been able to help her adjust to the crippling effects of her illness. Now he was bedridden, and she spoke of her gratitude that the Lord had empowered her with greater strength to be more self-reliant and better care for her own needs. She had even been given additional strength to minister to many of the needs of her dear companion, who had tenderly cared for her for so many years. Loving family and Church associates had also been helpful in assisting them so that they were able to remain in their own home with precious memories of earlier happy family associations.

It was President Spencer W. Kimball who said, "The Lord answers our prayers, but it is usually through another person that he meets our needs." An incident in the latter part of President Kimball's ministry helped me to better understand his message and the way his own life witnessed the truthfulness of his inspired counsel.

As a stake president during this period, I went to a local hospital to visit a dear sister suffering with a terminal illness. More than forty years earlier, I had attended school with both this sister and her husband, who had been childhood sweethearts. But they had not been blessed with children of their own, and they had filled this void by his serving as Scout leader—and his loving companion as the "Scout mother"—to scores of young boys over a generation.

As I approached the hospital that day, my heart was heavy with foreboding for what lay ahead in the lives of this couple. For weeks this dear brother had stayed with his companion at the hospital day and night to give comfort and ease her burden and the pain of her suffering.

As I reached the door of her hospital room that day, I met my friend emerging from his wife's room into the hallway. Unlike my earlier visits, when his countenance reflected the weight of their ordeal, this time his face was radiant and his eyes aglow. Before I could utter a word, he said, "You will never guess what just happened. As my wife and I were feeling so burdened, into our room came President Kimball"—himself a patient at the hospital, where he had recently undergone surgery. "He prayed with us and he blessed us, and it was as though the Savior himself had come to lift our burdens." Many other patients in that hospital, I might add, experienced a similar blessing from one who knew so much of pain and suffering.

In my own life I have experienced much of the Savior's love through the kindness and goodness of many of the Lord's servants. With King Benjamin I acknowledge that if we were to serve the Savior with all our souls, yet we would be unprofitable servants (Mosiah 2:21). And this because of the Savior's great love and atoning sacrifice for each of his children.

I have known men and women who, by their acts of service, are great examples of the "pure religion" described in the Epistle of James: "To visit the fatherless and widows in their affliction, and to keep [themselves] unspotted from the world" (James 1:27).

In these challenging times, dear brothers and sisters,

the need to "minister unto the least of these" of our Father's children is so great (see Matthew 25:40). How much we need the gifts of discernment and wisdom and charity to know how to truly reach down and lift our brothers and sisters to higher ground!

I pray that day by day we will strive more diligently to be about our Father's business (see Luke 2:49), to love and to serve our fellowmen—to feed the hungry, and clothe the naked, and comfort those that mourn (see Matthew 25:37–39), to hold up the hands that hang down, and to strengthen the feeble knees (see D&C 81:5)—to believe and live the Savior's doctrine, to follow after him and put first in our lives the things of his kingdom.

Index